Quick Mix Cakes

THE AUSTRALIAN
Women's Weekly

Contents

Tips & techniques 4

Large cakes 6

Small cakes 58

Loaf cakes 90

Glossary 116

Index 118

Conversion charts 120

We all love the wonderful smell of good things in the oven – perhaps none more so the perfect waft of cake cooking! To make a cake you will proud to serve, is not difficult and I hope that in following these recipes, you and your guests will enjoy the results. We have chosen recipes where the preparation time is 30 minutes and many of them, much less than this! Enjoy!

Pamela Clark

Food director

Tips & techniques

BAKING BASICS

How to best use your oven There are many different types of ovens and energy sources, so it's important that you get to know your oven – particularly when it comes to baking cakes. The recipes in this book were tested in domestic-sized electric fan-assisted ovens.

• If you're using a fan-assisted oven, check the operating instructions for best results. As a rule, reduce the temperature by 10°C to 20°C when using the fan during baking; recipes might also take slightly less time to bake than specified. Some ovens give better results if the fan is used for only part of the baking time; in this case, it is usually best to introduce the fan about halfway through.

• We positioned the oven racks and tins so that the top of the baked cake will be roughly in the centre of the oven. Best results are obtained by baking in an oven preheated to the desired temperature; this takes at least 10 minutes.

How to prepare a cake tin We prefer to use aluminium tins for baking whenever possible. Cake tins made

from materials with various coatings such as non-stick and the newer high-temperature silicone, work well provided the surface is unscratched. Tins made from tin and stainless steel do not conduct heat as evenly as aluminium. If using these tins, reduce the oven temperature by 10°C.

• To grease a cake tin, use either a light, even coating of cooking-oil spray, or a pastry brush to brush melted butter evenly over the base and side(s).

• To line a cake tin, trace around the base of the tin with a pencil onto baking parchment; cut out the shape, slightly inside the pencil mark, so that the paper fits snugly inside the greased tin. In most cases, it is not necessary to grease baking paper once it is in position.

• If you need to line the sides of a tin, make a baking parchment 'collar', extending it about 5cm above the edge of the tin, to protect the top of the cake. Cut a paper strip long enough to fit around inside of the tin and 8cm wider than the depth of the tin. Fold strip lengthways about 2cm from the edge and make short diagonal cuts about 2cm apart, up to the fold. This helps ease the paper around the curve of the tin, with cut section fitting around the base.

Position the paper circle over the base of the pan after lining sides.

To test if a cake is cooked All baking times are approximate. Check cake just after suggested time; it should be brown and starting to shrink from the side) of the tin. Feel the top with your fingertips; it should feel firm. You may want to insert a thin metal skewer into the deepest part of the cake from top to base. As the skewer is removed gently, it should have no uncooked mixture clinging to it. Do not confuse mixture with stickiness from fruit.

Cooling a cake We suggest standing a cake for up to 15 minutes before turning it onto a wire rack to cool. To turn out the cake, hold the tin firmly and shake it gently; this helps loosen the cake in the tin. Turn the cake, upside-down, onto a wire rack then turn the cake top-side up immediately using a second rack. Some wire racks can mark a cake, particularly a soft one such as a sponge. To prevent this, cover the rack with baking parchment.

• We have indicated when it is best to cool a cake in the tin; it is always covered with foil before cooling, and will usually be a fruit cake.

How to keep a cake Most cakes will keep well for two or three days depending on the type of cake; as a rule, remember that the higher the fat content, the longer a cake keeps.

• Cool the cake to room temperature before storing in an airtight container as close in size to the cake as possible.

• If a cake is suitable to freeze, it's best to do so unfilled and un-iced as icing can crack during the thawing process. A cake thaws best overnight in the refrigerator. Wrap or seal the cake in freezer wrap or freezer bags, expelling as much air as possible.

Cake-making Tips

• Use an electric beater to mix cakes, and always have the ingredients at room temperature, particularly the butter. Melted or extremely soft butter will alter the texture of the baked cake.

• Start mixing ingredients on a low speed; once the mixture is combined, increase the speed to about medium and beat for the required time.

• Creamed mixtures for cakes can be mixed with a wooden spoon, but this takes longer.

• When measuring liquids, always stand the marked measuring jug on a flat surface and check at eye level for accuracy.

• Spoon measurements should be levelled off with a knife or spatula.

WHAT WENT WRONG?

Sinks in centre on removal from oven Generally means the cake is undercooked.

Sinks in centre while still baking The oven is too hot.

Sugary crust Butter and sugar have not been creamed sufficiently.

White specks on top Undissolved sugar, or insufficient creaming.

Excessive shrinking The oven being too hot has caused cake to overcook.

Sticks to tin Too much sugar or other sweetening in recipe. If a recipe contains honey or syrup, or if you're using a new tin, line tin greased with greased baking parchment.

Crumbles when cut Mixture may have been creamed too much, or eggs added too quickly.

Rises and cracks in centre Cake tin too small or oven too hot (most cakes baked in loaf tins crack slightly).

Collar around top outside edge Cake baked at too high a temperature.

Pale on top, brown underneath and sides Too large a tin, or lining paper too high around sides of tin.

Uneven rising Oven shelf not straight, oven not level on floor, or mixture not spread evenly in tin.

Crusty, overbrowned, uncooked in centre Cake baked too long or at too high a temperature. Cake tin too small, causing top to overcook.

Fruit sinks to bottom Fruit not dried thoroughly; cake mixture too soft to support weight of the fruit (caused by over-creaming). Self-raising may have been used instead of plain flour. Fruit should be finely chopped so mixture can support it more easily.

Large Cakes

White chocolate & macadamia cake

preparation time 25 minutes **cooking time** 30 minutes **serves** 24

100g unsalted butter, chopped coarsely

400g white eating chocolate, chopped coarsely

¾ cup (165g) caster sugar

4 eggs

2 cups (300g) self raising flour

1 teaspoon vanilla extract

1 cup (140g) macadamia nuts, chopped finely

2 tablespoons icing sugar

1 Preheat oven to 170°C/150°C fan-assisted. Grease 22cm x 32cm baking tin; line base and two long sides with baking parchment, extending paper 5cm over sides.
2 Combine butter and chocolate in medium saucepan; stir over low heat until smooth. Remove from heat; stir in sugar. Cool 10 minutes.
3 Stir in eggs, then sifted flour, extract and nuts. Spread mixture into tin. Bake about 30 minutes. Cool in tin.
4 Turn cake, top-side up, onto board; dust with sifted icing sugar.

tip The cake can be made up to four days ahead; store in an airtight container.

Vanilla butter cake

preparation time 25 minutes **cooking time** 50 minutes (plus cooling time) **serves** 9

125g butter, chopped

¾ cup (180ml) milk

3 eggs

1 tablespoon vanilla extract

1 cup (220g) caster sugar

1½ cups (225g) self-raising flour

1. Preheat oven to 180°C/160°C fan-assisted. Grease deep 19cm-square cake tin; line base with baking parchment.
2. Stir butter and milk in small saucepan over heat until butter is melted. Remove from heat; cool to room temperature.
3. Beat eggs and extract in small bowl with electric mixer until thick and creamy; gradually add sugar, beat until dissolved between each addition. Transfer mixture to large bowl; stir in sifted flour and butter mixture, in two batches. Pour mixture into tin.
4. Bake cake about 45 minutes. Stand cake in tin 5 minutes; turn, top-side up, onto wire rack to cool. Dust cold cake with sifted icing sugar, if you like.

tip This cake can be stored in an airtight container for up to 3 days.

Genoise sponge

preparation time 20 minutes (plus standing time) **cooking time** 35 minutes (plus cooling time) **serves** 8

4 eggs

½ cup (110g) caster sugar

⅔ cup (100g) plain flour

60g butter, melted

300ml whipping cream

1 tablespoon icing sugar

¼ cup (80g) strawberry jam, warmed

500g strawberries, sliced thinly

1 tablespoon icing sugar, extra

1. Preheat oven to 180°C/160°C fan-assisted. Grease deep 20cm-round cake tin; line base with baking parchment.
2. Place eggs and caster sugar in large heatproof bowl over large saucepan simmering water. Do not allow water to touch base of bowl. Beat with electric mixer until thick and creamy, about 10 minutes. Remove bowl from pan; beat mixture until it returns to room temperature.
3. Sift half of the triple-sifted flour over egg mixture, carefully fold in flour; fold in remaining sifted flour. Quickly and carefully fold in cooled butter. Pour mixture into tin.
4. Bake sponge about 20 minutes. Turn, top-side up, onto baking-parchment-covered wire rack to cool.
5. Beat cream and sifted icing sugar in small bowl with electric mixer until soft peaks form. Split sponge in half; place one half, cut-side up, on serving plate. Spread with jam and cream; top with strawberries, then remaining sponge half. Dust with extra sifted icing sugar and strawberries, if you like.

tips Melted butter should be cooled to room temperature before being added. Unfilled cake can be frozen for up to 1 month.

Spiced sponge with pistachio honey cream

preparation time 20 minutes **cooking time** 18 minutes **serves** 10

4 eggs

¾ cup (165g) firmly packed dark brown sugar

1 cup (150g) cornflour

1 teaspoon cream of tartar

½ teaspoon bicarbonate of soda

1 teaspoon mixed spice

½ teaspoon ground cardamom

PISTACHIO HONEY CREAM

300ml whipping cream

1 tablespoon honey

¼ cup (30g) finely chopped roasted unsalted pistachios

1 Preheat oven to 180ºC/160ºC fan-assisted. Grease two deep 23cm-round cake tins.

2 Beat eggs and sugar in small bowl with electric mixer about 10 minutes or until sugar dissolves and mixture is thick and creamy; transfer to large bowl. Gently fold in triple-sifted dry ingredients.

3 Divide mixture between tins; bake about 18 minutes. Turn sponges, top-side up, onto baking-parchment-covered wire rack to cool.

4 Meanwhile, make pistachio honey cream. Sandwich sponges with cream; dust with a little sifted icing sugar.

PISTACHIO HONEY CREAM Beat cream and honey in small bowl with electric mixer until soft peaks form; fold in nuts.

Unless a recipe instructs you to do otherwise, use roasted unsalted nuts when making a cake since the butter you use has probably already had salt added to it. Buy the freshest nuts you can: they should taste slightly sweet. And be sure to taste any nuts you've had around for a while before using them to make certain they haven't gone rancid.

Cinnamon teacake

preparation time 15 minutes **cooking time** 30 minutes **serves** 8

60g butter, softened

1 teaspoon vanilla extract

⅔ cup (150g) caster sugar

1 egg

1 cup (150g) self-raising flour

⅓ cup (80ml) milk

10g butter, melted, extra

1 teaspoon ground cinnamon

1 tablespoon caster sugar, extra

1 Preheat oven to 180°C/160°C fan-assisted. Grease deep 20cm-round cake tin; line base with baking parchment.

2 Beat butter, extract, sugar and egg until light and fluffy. Stir in sifted flour and milk. Spread mixture into tin.

3 Bake cake about 30 minutes. Stand cake in tin 5 minutes; turn, top-side up, onto wire rack. Brush top of cake with melted butter, sprinkle with combined cinnamon and extra sugar.

tip This cake can be stored in an airtight container for up to 2 days.

Orange, almond & pine nut cake

preparation time 25 minutes **cooking time** 2 hours 30 minutes **serves** 16

2 medium oranges (480g)

1 teaspoon baking powder

6 eggs

1 cup (220g) caster sugar

2 cups (240g) ground almonds

½ cup (75g) plain flour

⅓ cup (50g) pine nuts

1 Place unpeeled whole oranges in medium saucepan, cover with cold water; bring to the boil. Boil, covered, 1½ hours or until oranges are tender; drain. Cool.

2 Preheat oven to 180°C/160°C fan-assisted. Grease deep 23cm-round cake tin; line base and side with baking parchment.

3 Trim and discard ends from oranges. Halve oranges; discard seeds. Blend or process oranges, including rind, with baking powder until mixture is pulpy.

4 Beat eggs and sugar in medium bowl with electric mixer about 5 minutes or until thick and creamy. Fold in ground almonds, sifted flour and orange pulp.

5 Pour mixture into tin, sprinkle with nuts; bake about 1 hour. Cool cake in tin.

large cakes

Carrot & banana cake

preparation time 20 minutes **cooking time** 1 hour 15 minutes (plus cooling time) **serves** 10

1¼ cups (185g) plain flour

½ cup (75g) self-raising flour

1 teaspoon bicarbonate of soda

1 teaspoon mixed spice

½ teaspoon ground cinnamon

1 cup (220g) firmly packed brown sugar

¾ cup (80g) coarsely chopped walnuts

3 eggs, beaten lightly

2 cups coarsely grated carrot

1 cup mashed banana

1 cup (250ml) vegetable oil

CREAM CHEESE FROSTING

90g cream cheese

90g butter

1 cup (160g) icing sugar

1 Preheat oven to 170°C/150°C fan-assisted. Grease base and side of 24cm-round springform tin; line base with baking parchment.
2 Sift flours, bicarbonate of soda, spices and sugar into large bowl. Stir in walnuts, egg, carrot, banana and oil; pour mixture into prepared tin.
3 Bake about 1¼ hours. Cool cake in tin.
4 Meanwhile, make cream cheese frosting.
5 Top cold cake with cream cheese frosting.
CREAM CHEESE FROSTING Beat cream cheese and butter in small bowl with electric mixer until as white as possible; gradually beat in icing sugar.

tips You will need about four medium carrots (480g) and two large overripe bananas (460g) for this recipe.
Pecans can be substituted for walnuts, if desired.

It is very important that the bananas you use are overripe; less-ripe ones won't mash easily and can cause the cake to be too heavy. A banana's natural starch is converted to sugar during the ripening process, and it's this natural sugar that contributes to the correct balance of ingredients. The cake also develops quite a thick crust because of this sugar content.

Lime & ricotta syrup cake

preparation time 15 minutes **cooking time** 1 hour **serves** 10

200g butter, softened

1 tablespoon finely grated lime rind

1 cup (220g) caster sugar

3 eggs, separated

250g ricotta cheese

½ cup (125ml) milk

1½ cups (225g) self-raising flour

LIME SYRUP

⅓ cup (80ml) lime juice

¼ cup (60ml) water

⅔ cup (150g) caster sugar

1 Preheat oven to 180ºC/160ºC fan-assisted. Grease 20cm baba pan well with melted butter.
2 Beat butter, rind and sugar in small bowl with electric mixer until light and fluffy. Beat in egg yolks, cheese and milk. Transfer to large bowl; stir in sifted flour.
3 Beat egg whites in small bowl with electric mixer until soft peaks form; fold into cheese mixture, in two batches.
4 Spread mixture into pan; bake about 1 hour. Stand cake in pan 5 minutes before turning onto wire rack set over tray.
5 Meanwhile, make lime syrup. Pour hot syrup over hot cake. Serve cake warm, with whipped cream, if you like.
   LIME SYRUP Stir ingredients in small saucepan over low heat until sugar dissolves; bring to the boil. Boil, uncovered, 2 minutes or until syrup thickens slightly.

   tip We used a 20cm (9-cup) silicone baba pan; a metal baba pan can also be used.

Greek yogurt cake

preparation time 25 minutes **cooking time** 35 minutes (plus cooling time) **serves** 12

125g butter, softened

1 cup (220g) caster sugar

3 eggs, separated

2 cups (300g) self-raising flour

½ teaspoon bicarbonate of soda

¼ cup (40g) finely chopped blanched almonds

1 cup (280g) plain Greek yogurt

1 Preheat oven to 180°C/160°C fan-assisted. Grease 20cm x 30cm baking tin; line base with baking parchment, extending paper 5cm over long sides.
2 Beat butter and sugar in small bowl with electric mixer until light and fluffy. Beat in egg yolks. Transfer mixture to large bowl; stir in sifted flour and soda in two batches. Stir in nuts and yogurt.
3 Beat egg whites in small bowl with electric mixer until soft peaks form. Fold egg whites into yogurt mixture, in two batches. Spread mixture into tin.
4 Bake cake about 35 minutes. Turn cake, top-side up, onto wire rack to cool. Dust with sifted icing sugar, if you like.

Matzo honey cake

preparation time 15 minutes **cooking time** 40 minutes **serves** 8

3 eggs, separated

1½ cups (180g) matzo flour

2 teaspoons finely grated orange rind

¼ teaspoon ground cloves

1 teaspoon ground cinnamon

⅔ cup (160ml) orange juice

¾ cup (270g) honey

½ cup (110g) firmly packed brown sugar

1 tablespoon icing sugar

1 Preheat oven to 180°C/160°C fan-assisted. Grease base of deep 22cm-round cake tin; line base with baking parchment.
2 Combine egg yolks, matzo flour, rind, spices, juice, honey and brown sugar in large bowl.
3 Beat egg whites in small bowl with electric mixer until soft peaks form; fold into matzo mixture, in two batches.
4 Pour cake mixture into tin; bake about 40 minutes. Stand cake 5 minutes; turn, top-side up, onto wire rack to cool.
5 Serve dusted with sifted icing sugar.

Matzo flour can be found in some supermarkets and delicatessens. If you can't find it, make your own by processing matzo crackers, biscuit-like unleavened bread, found in boxes on most supermarket shelves. It's important to use regular honey in the matzo cake, not the easy-to-pour liquefied version.

Pineapple coconut cake

preparation time 15 minutes **cooking time** 45 minutes **serves** 20

185g butter, softened

¾ cup (165g) caster sugar

3 eggs

⅔ cup (50g) desiccated coconut

1¾ cups (260g) self-raising flour

270ml can coconut cream

440g can crushed pineapple, well-drained

⅓ cup (25g) shredded coconut

LIME GLACÉ ICING

1½ cups (240g) icing sugar

20g butter, melted

2 tablespoons lime juice, approximately

1 Preheat oven to 180ºC/160ºC fan-assisted. Grease 22cm x 32cm rectangular cake tin; line base and sides with baking parchment, extending paper 5cm over edges.

2 Beat butter and sugar in small bowl with electric mixer until light and fluffy. Beat in eggs, one at a time. Transfer mixture to large bowl; stir in coconut, sifted flour, coconut cream and pineapple, in two batches.

3 Spread mixture into tin; bake 45 minutes. Stand cake in tin 10 minutes before turning, top-side up, onto wire rack to cool.

4 Meanwhile, make lime glacé icing; spread icing over cake, sprinkle with coconut.
LIME GLACÉ ICING Sift icing sugar into small heatproof bowl; stir in butter and enough of the juice to make a soft paste. Stir over small saucepan of simmering water until icing is spreadable.

Moist coconut cake with coconut ice frosting

preparation time 25 minutes **cooking time** 1 hour (plus cooling time) **serves** 10

125g butter, softened

½ teaspoon coconut essence

1 cup (220g) caster sugar

2 eggs

½ cup (40g) desiccated coconut

1½ cups (225g) self-raising flour

300g soured cream

⅓ cup (80ml) milk

COCONUT ICE FROSTING

2 cups (320g) icing sugar

1⅓ cups (110g) desiccated coconut

2 egg whites, beaten lightly

pink food colouring

1 Preheat oven to 180°C/160°C fan-assisted. Grease deep 22cm-round cake tin; line base with baking parchment.

2 Beat butter, essence and sugar in small bowl with electric mixer until light and fluffy. Beat in eggs, one at a time. Transfer mixture to large bowl; stir in coconut, sifted flour, soured cream and milk, in two batches. Spread mixture into tin.

3 Bake cake about 1 hour. Stand cake in tin 5 minutes; turn, top-side up, onto wire rack to cool.

4 Meanwhile, make coconut ice frosting.

5 Top cold cake with frosting; decorate with fresh raspberries if you prefer.
COCONUT ICE FROSTING Sift icing sugar into medium bowl; stir in coconut and egg whites. Tint pink with a little colouring.

Almond honey spice cake

preparation time 20 minutes **cooking time** 40 minutes (plus cooling, refrigeration and standing time) **serves** 10

125g butter, softened

⅓ cup (75g) caster sugar

2 tablespoons honey

1 teaspoon ground ginger

1 teaspoon ground allspice

2 eggs

1½ cups (180g) ground almonds

½ cup (80g) semolina

1 teaspoon baking powder

¼ cup (60ml) milk

SPICED SYRUP

1 cup (220g) caster sugar

1 cup (250ml) water

8 cardamom pods, bruised

2 cinnamon sticks

HONEY ORANGE CREAM

¾ cup (180ml) whipping cream

1 tablespoon honey

2 tablespoons finely grated orange rind

1 Preheat oven to 180°C/160°C fan-assisted. Grease deep 20cm-round cake tin; line base and side with baking parchment.

2 Beat butter, sugar, honey and spices in small bowl with electric mixer until light and fluffy. Add eggs, one at a time, beating until just combined between additions; transfer mixture to medium bowl. Fold in ground almonds, semolina, baking powder and milk.

3 Spread mixture into tin; bake about 40 minutes. Stand cake in tin 5 minutes.

4 Meanwhile, make spiced syrup.

5 Pour strained hot syrup over hot cake in tin; cool cake in tin to room temperature. Turn cake, in tin, upside-down onto serving plate; refrigerate 3 hours or overnight.

6 Remove cake from refrigerator. Make honey orange cream. Remove tin from cake; serve cake at room temperature with honey orange cream.

SPICED SYRUP Stir ingredients in small saucepan over heat, without boiling, until sugar dissolves; bring to a boil. Boil, uncovered, without stirring, about 5 minutes or until syrup thickens slightly.

HONEY ORANGE CREAM Beat cream, honey and rind in small bowl with electric mixer until soft peaks form.

Syrup cakes almost always have hot syrup poured over them when they're hot. Sometimes the syrup is poured over them while they're still in their cake tins, sometimes the cakes are turned out. In this case, the wire rack has a tray placed under it to catch the drips of syrup. This overflow should be poured back over the cake.

Honey spice sponge cake

preparation time 15 minutes **cooking time** 10 minutes **serves** 6

2 eggs

½ cup (110g) caster sugar

⅓ cup (50g) cornflour

1½ tablespoons custard powder

1 teaspoon mixed spice

½ teaspoon cream of tartar

¼ teaspoon bicarbonate of soda

300ml whipping cream

2 tablespoons honey

1 tablespoon icing sugar

1 Preheat oven to 180°C/160°C fan-assisted. Grease 25cm x 30cm swiss roll tin; line base with baking parchment, extending paper 5cm over long sides.

2 Beat eggs and ⅓ cup of the sugar in small bowl with electric mixer about 10 minutes or until thick and creamy.

3 Meanwhile, triple-sift cornflour, custard powder, spice, cream of tartar and soda onto baking parchment. Sift flour mixture over egg mixture; fold ingredients together. Spread mixture into tin; bake 10 minutes.

4 Place a piece of baking parchment cut the same size as tin on bench; sprinkle evenly with remaining sugar. Turn cake onto sugared paper; peel lining paper away. Cool.

5 Beat cream and honey in small bowl with electric mixer until firm peaks form.

6 Cut edges from all sides of sponge then cut widthways into three rectangles. Place one piece of sponge on plate; spread with half the cream mixture. Top with second piece of sponge and remaining cream. Finish with remaining piece sponge and dust with sifted icing sugar.

Moist orange cake

preparation time 25 minutes **cooking time** 45 minutes (plus cooling time) **serves** 8

155g butter, softened

2 teaspoons finely grated orange rind

⅔ cup (150g) caster sugar

3 eggs

1¼ cups (185g) self-raising flour

¼ cup (60ml) milk

1 tablespoon desiccated coconut

ORANGE ICING

1 cup (160g) icing sugar

1 teaspoon butter, softened

1 tablespoon orange juice, approximately

1 Preheat oven to 180°C/160°C fan-assisted. Grease deep 20cm-round cake tin; line base with baking parchment.

2 Combine butter, rind, sugar, eggs, sifted flour and milk in large bowl; beat on low speed with electric mixer until combined. Increase speed to medium, beat about 3 minutes or until mixture is lighter in colour and smooth.

3 Spread mixture into tin; bake about 45 minutes. Stand cake in tin 5 minutes before turning onto wire rack to cool.

4 Meanwhile, make orange icing.

5 Spread cold cake with orange icing; sprinkle with coconut.
   ORANGE ICING Sift icing sugar into small heatproof bowl, stir in butter and enough juice to make a stiff paste. Stir over hot water until icing is spreadable.

tip Can be made two days ahead; keep in an airtight container.

Caramelised apple butter cake

preparation time 20 minutes **cooking time** 1 hour **serves** 10

2 medium apples (300g)

80g butter

¾ cup (165g) firmly packed brown sugar

125g butter, softened, extra

⅔ cup (150g) caster sugar

1 teaspoon vanilla extract

2 eggs

1 cup (150g) self-raising flour

⅔ cup (100g) plain flour

½ teaspoon bicarbonate of soda

1 cup (250ml) buttermilk

¾ cup (180ml) double cream

1 Preheat oven to 180°C/160°C fan-assisted. Grease 20cm ring tin.

2 Peel, core and quarter apples; slice thinly. Melt butter in large frying pan; cook apple about 5 minutes or until browned lightly. Add brown sugar; cook, stirring, about 5 minutes or until mixture thickens slightly. Strain apples over medium bowl. Reserve apples and cooking liquid.

3 Beat extra butter, caster sugar and extract in small bowl with electric mixer until light and fluffy. Add eggs, one at a time, beating until just combined between additions; transfer to large bowl. Stir in sifted dry ingredients and buttermilk, in two batches.

4 Spread two-thirds of the mixture into tin. Top with apples, leaving a 2cm border around the edge; cover with remaining mixture. Bake about 50 minutes. Stand cake 5 minutes; turn, top-side up, onto wire rack to cool.

5 Meanwhile, return reserved apple liquid to large frying pan, add cream; bring to a boil. Reduce heat; simmer, uncovered, about 15 minutes or until sauce thickens.

6 Serve warm cake with caramel sauce.

We used the Golden Delicious variety for this recipe, a crisp, almost citrus-coloured apple with excellent flavour and good keeping properties. It's probably the best cooking apple around, but you can substitute it with green-skinned Granny Smiths if you prefer.

large cakes

Rich chocolate cake

preparation time 15 minutes **cooking time** 1 hour 30 minutes (plus cooling time) **serves** 8

185g butter

2 teaspoons vanilla essence

1¾ cups (385g) caster sugar

3 eggs

2 cups (300g) self-raising flour

⅔ cup (70g) cocoa powder

1 cup (250ml) water

CHOCOLATE ICING

90g dark chocolate, chopped coarsely

30g butter

1 cup (160g) icing sugar

2 tablespoons hot water, approximately

1 Preheat oven to 180°C/160°C fan-assisted. Grease base and side of deep 23cm-round cake tin; line base with baking parchment.

2 Combine butter, essence, sugar, eggs, flour, cocoa and the water in large bowl; beat on low speed using electric mixer until ingredients are combined. Increase speed to medium; beat about 3 minutes or until mixture is smooth and changed in colour. Spread into prepared tin.

3 Bake cake 1½ hours. Stand 5 minutes, then turn onto wire rack to cool. Spread with chocolate icing.
CHOCOLATE ICING Melt chocolate and butter in medium bowl over hot water; gradually stir in sifted icing sugar, then stir in enough of the water to mix to a spreadable consistency.

tip Chocolate cake can be stored in airtight container 3 days.

Marble cake

preparation time 25 minutes (plus cooling time) **cooking time** 1 hour **serves** 12

250g butter, softened

1 teaspoon vanilla extract

1¼ cups (275g) caster sugar

3 eggs

2¼ cups (335g) self-raising flour

¾ cup (180ml) milk

pink food colouring

2 tablespoons cocoa powder

2 tablespoons milk, extra

BUTTER FROSTING

90g butter, softened

1 cup (160g) icing sugar

1 tablespoon milk

1 Preheat oven to 180°C/160°C fan-assisted. Grease deep 22cm-round cake tin; line with baking parchment.

2 Beat butter, extract and sugar in medium bowl with electric mixer until light and fluffy. Beat in eggs, one at a time. Stir in sifted flour and milk, in two batches.

3 Divide mixture among three bowls; tint one mixture pink. Blend sifted cocoa with extra milk in cup; stir into second mixture. Drop alternate spoonfuls of mixtures into tin. Pull a skewer backwards and forwards through cake mixture.

4 Bake cake about 1 hour. Stand cake in tin 5 minutes; turn, top-side up, onto wire rack to cool.

5 Meanwhile, make butter frosting.

6 Top marble cake with butter frosting.
BUTTER FROSTING Beat butter in small bowl with electric mixer until light and fluffy; beat in sifted icing sugar and milk, in two batches. Tint pink with colouring.

tip This cake can be stored, at room temperature, in an airtight container for 2 days, or can be frozen for 2 months.

large cakes

Lime & poppy seed syrup cake

preparation time 20 minutes **cooking time** 1 hour **serves** 16

¼ cup (40g) poppy seeds

½ cup (125ml) milk

250g butter, softened

1 tablespoon finely grated lime rind

1¼ cups (275g) caster sugar

4 eggs

2¼ cups (335g) self-raising flour

¾ cup (110g) plain flour

1 cup (240g) soured cream

LIME SYRUP

½ cup (125ml) lime juice

1 cup (250ml) water

1 cup (220g) caster sugar

1 Preheat oven to 180°C/160°C fan-assisted. Grease base and sides of deep 23cm-square cake tin.

2 Combine poppy seeds and milk in small jug; soak 10 minutes.

3 Beat butter, rind and sugar in small bowl with electric mixer until light and fluffy. Add eggs, one at a time, beating until combined between additions; transfer mixture to large bowl. Stir in sifted flours, cream and poppy seed mixture, in two batches.

4 Spread mixture into tin; bake about 1 hour.

5 Meanwhile, make lime syrup.

6 Stand cake in tin 5 minutes, turn onto wire rack over tray. Pour hot lime syrup over hot cake.

LIME SYRUP Combine ingredients in small saucepan. Stir over heat, without boiling, until sugar dissolves. Simmer, uncovered, without stirring, 5 minutes.

Before grating the lime, make sure it is at room temperature and roll it, pressing down hard with your hand, on the kitchen bench. This will help extract as much juice as possible from the fruit. You can substitute the same weight of other citrus fruit – lemons mandarins, blood oranges, oranges, etc – for the limes if you wish.

Ginger cake with caramel icing

preparation time 25 minutes **cooking time** 1 hour **serves** 10

¾ cup (165g) firmly packed brown sugar

¾ cup (110g) plain flour

½ cup (75g) self-raising flour

½ teaspoon bicarbonate of soda

2 teaspoons ground ginger

1 teaspoon ground cinnamon

½ teaspoon ground nutmeg

125g butter, softened

2 eggs

⅔ cup (160ml) buttermilk

CARAMEL ICING

60g butter

½ cup (110g) firmly packed brown sugar

2 tablespoons milk

¾ cup (120g) icing sugar

1 Preheat oven to 170ºC/150ºC fan-assisted. Grease deep 20cm ring cake tin.

2 Sift dry ingredients into medium bowl. Add remaining ingredients; beat with electric mixer on low speed until ingredients are combined. Increase speed to medium; beat about 2 minutes or until mixture is smooth and paler in colour.

3 Pour mixture into tin; bake about 35 minutes. Stand cake in tin 10 minutes before turning, top-side up, onto wire rack to cool.

4 Meanwhile, make caramel icing. Drizzle warm icing over cake. **CARAMEL ICING** Stir butter, brown sugar and milk in small saucepan over heat until sugar dissolves; bring to the boil then simmer, stirring, 2 minutes. Remove pan from heat, stir in sifted icing sugar.

tip This cake will almost certainly crack, as most ring-shaped cakes do; however, the icing will cover any cracks.

Mandarin, polenta & macadamia cake

preparation time 20 minutes (plus cooling time) **cooking time** 2 hours (plus standing time) **serves** 10

4 small mandarins (400g), unpeeled

2 cups (280g) macadamias

250g butter, softened

1 teaspoon vanilla extract

1 cup (220g) caster sugar

3 eggs

1 cup (170g) polenta

1 teaspoon baking powder

1 tablespoon icing sugar

1 Cover whole mandarins in medium saucepan with cold water; bring to a boil. Drain then repeat process two more times. Cool mandarins to room temperature.

2 Preheat oven to moderately slow (170°C/150°C fan-assisted). Grease deep 22cm-round cake pan; line base with baking parchment.

3 Blend or process nuts until mixture forms a coarse meal. Halve mandarins; discard seeds. Blend or process mandarins until pulpy.

4 Beat butter, extract and caster sugar in small bowl with electric mixer until light and fluffy. Add eggs, one at a time, beating until just combined between additions; transfer to large bowl. Stir in polenta, baking powder, nut meal and mandarin pulp.

5 Spread mixture into pan; bake about 1 hour. Stand cake 15 minutes; turn, top-side up, onto wire rack to cool. Serve cake dusted with sifted icing sugar.

Whipped cream cake with caramel frosting

preparation time 20 minutes **cooking time** 50 minutes **serves** 10

600ml whipping cream

3 eggs

1 teaspoon vanilla extract

1¼ cups (275g) firmly packed brown sugar

2 cups (300g) self-raising flour

CARAMEL FROSTING

60g butter

½ cup (110g) firmly packed brown sugar

2 tablespoons milk

½ cup (80g) icing sugar

1 Preheat oven to 180°C/160°C fan-assisted. Grease deep 22cm-round cake tin; line base with baking parchment.

2 Beat half of the cream in small bowl with electric mixer until soft peaks form. Beat eggs and extract in small bowl with electric mixer until thick and creamy; gradually add sugar, beating until dissolved between additions.

3 Transfer mixture to large bowl. Fold in a quarter of the whipped cream then sifted flour, then remaining whipped cream. Spread into tin; bake about 50 minutes. Stand cake 5 minutes; turn, top-side up, onto wire rack to cool.

4 Meanwhile, beat remaining cream in small bowl with electric mixer until firm peaks form.

5 Make caramel frosting.

6 Split cold cake in half; sandwich layers with cream. Spread top of cake with caramel frosting.
CARAMEL FROSTING Melt butter in small saucepan, add brown sugar and milk; bring to a boil. Reduce heat immediately; simmer 2 minutes. Cool to room temperature. Stir in icing sugar until smooth.

In this recipe, cream replaces milk and butter, resulting in a cake that's firm like a buttercake – even though it's made like a sponge.

Passionfruit buttermilk cake

preparation time 20 minutes cooking time 45 minutes (plus cooling time) serves 12

250g butter, softened

1 cup (220g) caster sugar

3 eggs, separated

2 cups (300g) self-raising flour

¾ cup (180ml) buttermilk

¼ cup (60ml) passionfruit pulp

PASSIONFRUIT ICING

1½ cups (240g) icing sugar

¼ cup (60ml) passionfruit pulp, approximately

1 Preheat oven to 180°C/160°C fan-assisted. Grease and lightly flour 24cm ring tin; tap out excess flour.

2 Beat butter and sugar in small bowl with electric mixer until light and fluffy. Beat in egg yolks, one at a time. Transfer mixture to large bowl; stir in sifted flour, buttermilk and passionfruit, in two batches.

3 Beat egg whites in small bowl with electric mixer until soft peaks form. Fold into cake mixture, in two batches. Spread mixture into tin.

4 Bake cake about 40 minutes. Stand cake in tin 5 minutes; turn onto wire rack to cool.

5 Meanwhile, make passionfruit icing; drizzle over cold cake.
   PASSIONFRUIT ICING Sift icing sugar into small heatproof bowl; stir in enough passionfruit pulp to form a firm paste. Stand bowl over small saucepan of simmering water, stir until icing is a pouring consistency (do not overheat).

tip You could bake this cake in a deep 22cm-round cake tin; it will take about 1 hour to cook.

Berry cake with vanilla bean syrup

preparation time 20 minutes cooking time 40 minutes serves 8

125g butter, chopped

1 cup (220g) caster sugar

3 eggs

½ cup (75g) plain flour

¼ cup (35g) self-raising flour

½ cup (60g) ground almonds

⅓ cup (80g) soured cream

1½ cups (225g) frozen mixed berries

½ cup (100g) drained canned pitted black cherries

VANILLA BEAN SYRUP

½ cup (125ml) water

½ cup (110g) caster sugar

2 vanilla pods

1 Preheat oven to 180°C/160°C fan-assisted. Grease 20cm baba pan thoroughly.

2 Beat butter and sugar in small bowl with electric mixer until light and fluffy. Beat in eggs, one at a time. (Mixture will curdle at this stage, but will come together later.) Transfer mixture to large bowl; stir in sifted flours, ground almonds, soured cream, berries and cherries. Pour mixture into pan.

3 Bake cake about 40 minutes.

4 Meanwhile, make vanilla bean syrup.

5 Stand cake in pan 5 minutes; turn onto wire rack placed over large tray. Pour hot syrup over hot cake.
   VANILLA BEAN SYRUP Combine the water and sugar in small saucepan. Split vanilla pods in half lengthways; scrape seeds into pan then add pods. Stir over heat, without boiling, until sugar dissolves. Simmer, uncovered, without stirring, 5 minutes. Using tongs, remove pods from syrup.

large cakes

Passionfruit & lemon syrup cake

preparation time 20 minutes **cooking time** 1 hour **serves** 16

⅔ cup (160ml) passionfruit pulp

250g butter, softened

1 tablespoon finely grated lemon rind

1 cup (220g) caster sugar

3 eggs

1 cup (250ml) buttermilk

2 cups (300g) self-raising flour

LEMON SYRUP

⅓ cup (80ml) lemon juice

¼ cup (60ml) water

¾ cup (165g) caster sugar

1   Preheat oven to 180°C/160°C fan-assisted. Grease deep 19cm-square cake tin well; line base and sides with baking parchment.
2   Strain passionfruit over medium jug; reserve both juice and seeds.
3   Beat butter, rind and sugar in small bowl with electric mixer until light and fluffy. Add eggs, one at a time, beating until combined between additions; transfer to large bowl.
4   Fold in combined passionfruit juice and buttermilk, and sifted flour, in two batches. Spread mixture into tin; bake about 1 hour.
5   Meanwhile, make lemon syrup.
6   Stand cake 5 minutes; turn, top-side up, onto wire rack set over tray. Pour hot syrup over hot cake; serve warm.
    LEMON SYRUP Combine juice, the water, sugar and half of the reserved passionfruit seeds (discard remaining seeds or freeze for future use) in small saucepan; stir over heat, without boiling, until sugar dissolves. Simmer, uncovered, without stirring, 5 minutes.

A passionfruit is well-named: the fruit's simultaneously sweet and tart taste inspires an almost addictive passion in the person savouring its seedy, yellow pulp. Its singular flavour marries well with yogurt and creamy desserts like panna cotta, ice-cream or bavarois. You will require about seven passionfruits for this recipe.

Muscat prune shortcake

preparation time 25 minutes **cooking time** 25 minutes (plus cooling and refrigeration time) **serves** 10

200g butter, softened

1 teaspoon finely grated lemon rind

⅓ cup (75g) caster sugar

¼ cup (50g) rice flour

¾ cup (110g) self-raising flour

¾ cup (110g) plain flour

300ml whipping cream

1 tablespoon caster sugar, extra

MUSCAT PRUNES

1 cup (170g) pitted prunes, chopped coarsely

1 cup (250ml) muscat

1 Preheat oven to 180°C/160°C fan-forced. Grease three 20cm-round sandwich tins.

2 Beat butter, rind and sugar in medium bowl with electric mixer until light and fluffy. Fold in sifted flours, in two batches.

3 Press mixture evenly into tins; bake about 20 minutes. Stand shortcakes in tins; cool to room temperature.

4 Meanwhile, make muscat prunes.

5 Beat cream in small bowl with electric mixer until firm peaks form. Place one shortcake into deep 20cm-round cake tin or 20cm springform tin; spread with half of the prune mixture then half of the whipped cream. Top with another shortcake; spread with remaining prune mixture then remaining whipped cream. Top with remaining shortcake, cover; refrigerate overnight.

6 Remove from tin; serve sprinkled with extra sugar.
   MUSCAT PRUNES Stir prunes and muscat in small saucepan over heat, without boiling, until prunes soften. Cool to room temperature.

A fortified wine, like sherry and port, muscat is the result of grapes left to ripen well beyond normal harvesting time, resulting in a concentrated dark, toffee-coloured wine with a rich yet mellow flavour, equally good used in cooking as it is as an after-dinner drink.

Maple pecan cake

preparation time 15 minutes **cooking time** 1 hour **serves** 10

cooking-oil spray

1 cup (100g) pecans

⅓ cup (80ml) maple syrup

1¼ cups (235g) coarsely chopped dried figs

1 teaspoon bicarbonate of soda

1¼ cups (310ml) boiling water

60g butter

¾ cup (150g) firmly packed brown sugar

2 eggs

1 cup (150g) self-raising flour

MAPLE BUTTERSCOTCH SAUCE

1 cup (250ml) maple syrup

½ cup (125ml) double cream

100g butter, chopped

1 Preheat oven to 180°C/160°C fan-assisted. Grease deep 20cm-round cake tin; line base with baking parchment. Spray paper with oil.
2 Arrange nuts over base of tin; drizzle with maple syrup.
3 Place figs, bicarbonate of soda and the water in bowl of food processor; cover with lid, stand 5 minutes. Add butter and sugar; process until almost smooth. Add eggs and flour; process until just combined. Pour mixture into tin.
4 Bake cake about 55 minutes. Stand cake in tin 5 minutes; turn onto wire rack to cool.
5 Meanwhile, make maple butterscotch sauce.
6 Serve cake with sauce and, if you like, vanilla ice-cream.
MAPLE BUTTERSCOTCH SAUCE Stir ingredients in small saucepan over heat until smooth; bring to the boil. Boil, uncovered, about 2 minutes or until mixture thickens slightly.

tip You can use either pure maple syrup or maple-flavoured syrup in this recipe.

Fig, pecan & maple syrup cake

preparation time 20 minutes **cooking time** 40 minutes **serves** 8

125g butter, softened

½ cup (110g) firmly packed brown sugar

4 eggs, separated

1½ cups (180g) ground pecans (see tip)

⅓ cup (55g) semolina

¼ cup (60ml) milk

1 cup (200g) finely chopped dried figs

MAPLE SYRUP

½ cup (125ml) maple syrup

⅓ cup (75g) firmly packed brown sugar

½ cup (125ml) water

1 Preheat oven to 180ºC/160ºC fan-assisted. Grease deep 23cm-round cake tin; line base and side with baking parchment.
2 Beat butter and sugar in small bowl with electric mixer until light and fluffy; beat in egg yolks. Transfer mixture to large bowl; stir in ground pecans and semolina, then milk and figs.
3 Beat egg whites in small bowl with electric mixer until soft peaks form; fold into fig mixture, in two batches. Pour mixture into tin; bake about 40 minutes.
4 Meanwhile, make maple syrup.
5 Stand cake in tin 5 minutes before turning, top-side up, onto wire rack set over tray. Pour hot syrup over hot cake. Serve cake warm.
MAPLE SYRUP Stir ingredients in small saucepan over low heat until sugar dissolves; bring to the boil. Boil, uncovered, about 5 minutes or until thickened slightly.

tips You will need to blend about 240g pecans to get enough ground pecans for this recipe. The semolina can be replaced with 50g plain flour.

Lemon sour cream cake

preparation time 15 minutes **cooking time** 1 hour (plus cooling time) **serves** 16

250g butter, softened

1 tablespoon finely grated lemon rind

2 cups (440g) caster sugar

6 eggs

¾ cup (180g) soured cream

2 cups (300g) plain flour

¼ cup (35g) self-raising flour

½ cup (80g) pine nuts

1 tablespoon demerara sugar

¼ cup (90g) honey

1 Preheat oven to 170°C/150°C fan-assisted. Grease deep 23cm-square cake tin; line base and two opposite sides with baking parchment, extending paper 5cm over sides.

2 Beat butter, rind and caster sugar in medium bowl with electric mixer until light and fluffy. Add eggs, one at a time, beating until just combined between additions (mixture might separate at this stage, but will come together later). Stir in soured cream and sifted flours, in two batches. Spread mixture into tin; bake 15 minutes.

3 Meanwhile, combine pine nuts and demerara sugar in small bowl.

4 Carefully remove cake from oven; working quickly, sprinkle evenly with nut mixture, press gently into cake. Return cake to oven; bake further 45 minutes. Stand cake 5 minutes; turn, top-side up, onto wire rack.

5 Meanwhile, heat honey in small saucepan. Drizzle hot cake evenly with hot honey; cool before serving.

There are several varieties of pine tree that produce nuts large enough to be harvested for use in cooking, but the best are those from the stone pine, a tree grown around the Mediterranean. Shaped rather like an elongated torpedo, this particularly buttery pine nut is superior in flavour to the cheaper Asian-grown variety.

Flourless hazelnut chocolate cake

preparation time 20 minutes (plus standing time) **cooking time** 1 hour **serves** 9

⅓ cup (35g) cocoa powder

⅓ cup (80ml) hot water

150g dark eating chocolate, melted

150g butter, melted

1⅓ cups (275g) firmly packed brown sugar

1 cup (100g) ground hazelnuts

4 eggs, separated

1 tablespoon cocoa powder, extra

1 Preheat oven to 180°C/160°C fan-assisted. Grease deep 19cm-square cake tin; line base and sides with baking parchment.

2 Blend cocoa with the hot water in large bowl until smooth. Stir in chocolate, butter, sugar, ground hazelnuts and egg yolks.

3 Beat egg whites in small bowl with electric mixer until soft peaks form; fold into chocolate mixture in two batches. Pour mixture into tin.

4 Bake cake about 1 hour or until firm. Stand cake in tin 15 minutes; turn, top-side up, onto wire rack to cool. Dust with sifted extra cocoa.

tips This cake can be made up to 4 days ahead and refrigerated, covered. It can also be frozen for up to 3 months.
Ground hazelnuts, also sold as hazelnut meal, is a flour-like substance made after the nuts have been roasted.

Rich chocolate hazelnut cake

preparation time 20 minutes **cooking time** 1 hour 30 minutes **serves** 8

150g unsalted butter, chopped coarsely

150g dark eating chocolate, chopped coarsely

5 eggs, separated

⅔ cup (150g) caster sugar

1½ cups (150g) ground hazelnuts

⅓ cup (45g) roasted hazelnuts, chopped coarsely

DARK CHOCOLATE GANACHE

⅓ cup (80ml) whipping cream

100g dark eating chocolate, chopped coarsely

1 Preheat oven to 160°C/140°C fan-assisted. Grease deep 20cm-round cake tin; line base and sides with baking parchment.

2 Combine butter and chocolate in small saucepan; stir over low heat until smooth. Cool 10 minutes.

3 Beat egg yolks and sugar in medium bowl with electric mixer until thick and pale; beat in chocolate mixture. Beat egg whites in small bowl with electric mixer until soft peaks form. Fold ground hazelnuts into chocolate mixture, then fold in egg white, in two batches. Spoon mixture into tin; bake about 1½ hours.

4 Cool cake in tin. Turn cake, top-side down, onto serving plate.

5 Meanwhile, make dark chocolate ganache.

6 Spread cake with ganache; top with nuts.
DARK CHOCOLATE GANACHE Bring cream to the boil in small saucepan. Remove from heat, add chocolate; stir until smooth. Stand 5 minutes before using.

tips The cake can be made a week ahead; keep, covered, in the refrigerator. Make and use the ganache a day before serving.

Chocolate mud cake with chilli cherries

preparation time 25 minutes **cooking time** 1 hour 35 minutes (plus cooling time) **serves** 10

250g butter, chopped

200g dark eating chocolate, chopped coarsely

2 cups (440g) caster sugar

1 cup (250ml) milk

1 teaspoon vanilla extract

⅓ cup (80ml) bourbon

1½ cups (225g) plain flour

¼ cup (35g) self-raising flour

¼ cup (25g) cocoa powder

2 eggs

DARK CHOCOLATE GANACHE

⅓ cup (80ml) double cream

200g dark eating chocolate

CHILLI CHERRIES

2 cups (500ml) water

¾ cup (165g) caster sugar

1 fresh red thai chilli, halved lengthways

1 star anise

6 whole black peppercorns

10cm piece orange peel

300g frozen cherries

1 Preheat oven to 170°C/150°C fan-assisted. Grease deep 22cm-round cake tin; line base with baking parchment.

2 Combine butter, chocolate, sugar, milk, extract and bourbon in medium saucepan; stir over low heat until smooth. Transfer to large bowl; cool 15 minutes. Whisk in sifted flours and cocoa, then eggs.

3 Pour mixture into tin; bake about 1 hour 30 minutes.

4 Meanwhile, make chilli cherries.

5 Stand cake 5 minutes; turn, top-side up, onto wire rack to cool.

6 Meanwhile, make dark chocolate ganache.

7 Spread cold cake with ganache; serve with chilli cherries.

DARK CHOCOLATE GANACHE Bring cream to a boil in small saucepan. Remove from heat; add chocolate, stir until smooth.

CHILLI CHERRIES Stir the water, sugar, chilli, star anise, peppercorns and peel in medium saucepan over low heat, without boiling, until sugar dissolves. Bring to a boil; boil 2 minutes. Add cherries; simmer 5 minutes or until cherries are just tender. Cool cherries in syrup. Remove cherries from pan; bring syrup to a boil. Boil 10 minutes or until syrup thickens slightly; cool. Return cherries to pan.

The Aztecs first combined chocolate and chilli about 2600 years ago, and eating the chilli cherries with bites of this rich dark cake will confirm that the two tastes do indeed complement one another. Use your favourite whisky instead of bourbon, if you prefer. Fresh or canned cherries can replace the frozen variety, if necessary. Use the drained cherries' syrup to replace an equal amount of the required two cups of water.

Family chocolate cake

preparation time 20 minutes **cooking time** 50 minutes (plus cooling time) **serves** 20

2 cups (500ml) water

3 cups (660g) caster sugar

250g butter, chopped

⅓ cup (35g) cocoa powder

1 teaspoon bicarbonate of soda

3 cups (450g) self-raising flour

4 eggs

FUDGE FROSTING

90g butter

⅓ cup (80ml) water

½ cup (110g) caster sugar

1½ cups (240g) icing sugar

⅓ cup (35g) cocoa powder

1 Preheat oven to 180°C/160°C fan-assisted. Grease deep 26.5cm x 33cm (3.5-litre) baking tin; line base with baking parchment.

2 Combine the water, sugar, butter and sifted cocoa and soda in medium saucepan; stir over heat, without boiling, until sugar dissolves. Bring to a boil then reduce heat; simmer, uncovered, 5 minutes. Transfer mixture to large bowl; cool to room temperature.

3 Add flour and eggs to bowl; beat with electric mixer until mixture is smooth and pale in colour. Pour mixture into tin; bake about 50 minutes. Stand cake 10 minutes; turn, top-side up, onto wire rack to cool.

4 Spread cold cake with fudge frosting.
   FUDGE FROSTING Combine butter, the water and caster sugar in small saucepan; stir over low heat, without boiling, until sugar dissolves. Sift icing sugar and cocoa into small bowl then gradually stir in hot butter mixture. Cover; refrigerate about 20 minutes or until frosting thickens. Beat with wooden spoon until spreadable.

Chocolate blueberry slab cake

preparation time 20 minutes **cooking time** 50 minutes (plus cooling time) **serves** 20

½ cup (50g) cocoa powder

½ cup (125ml) boiling water

160g unsalted butter, softened

1½ cups (330g) caster sugar

3 eggs

1⅓ cups (200g) self-raising flour

⅓ cup (50g) plain flour

½ teaspoon bicarbonate of soda

¾ cup (180ml) buttermilk

⅔ cup (100g) fresh blueberries

CHOCOLATE FROSTING

100g dark cooking chocolate, chopped coarsely

25g butter

1 cup (160g) icing sugar, sifted

1½ tablespoons hot water

1 Preheat oven to 180°C/160°C fan-assisted. Grease 19cm x 30cm baking tin; line with baking parchment.

2 Blend cocoa with the water in small bowl. Cool.

3 Beat butter and sugar in small bowl with electric mixer until light and fluffy. Beat in eggs, one at a time. Transfer mixture to large bowl, stir in sifted flours and soda, and buttermilk in two batches; stir in cocoa mixture.

4 Spread mixture into tin. Bake about 30 minutes. Cool cake in tin 20 minutes before turning, top-side up, onto wire rack to cool.

5 Make chocolate frosting.

6 Spread cold cake with frosting; top with blueberries.
   CHOCOLATE FROSTING Melt chocolate and butter in small saucepan, stirring, over low heat. Remove from heat; stir in sifted icing sugar and water until smooth.

Lemon & lime white chocolate mud cake

preparation time 20 minutes **cooking time** 1 hour 50 minutes (plus cooling and refrigeration time) **serves** 8

250g butter, chopped

2 teaspoons finely grated lemon rind

2 teaspoons finely grated lime rind

180g white eating chocolate, chopped coarsely

1½ cups (330g) caster sugar

¾ cup (180ml) milk

1½ cups (225g) plain flour

½ cup (75g) self-raising flour

2 eggs, beaten lightly

COCONUT GANACHE

140ml can coconut cream

360g white eating chocolate, chopped finely

1 teaspoon finely grated lemon rind

1 teaspoon finely grated lime rind

1 Preheat oven to 170°C/150°C fan-assisted. Grease deep 20cm-round cake tin; line base with baking parchment.

2 Combine butter, rinds, chocolate, sugar and milk in medium saucepan; stir over low heat until smooth. Transfer mixture to large bowl; cool 15 minutes.

3 Stir in sifted flours and egg; pour mixture into tin. Bake about 1 hour 40 minutes; cool cake in tin.

4 Meanwhile, make coconut ganache.

5 Turn cake, top-side up, onto serving plate; spread ganache over cooled cake.

COCONUT GANACHE Bring coconut cream to a boil in small saucepan; combine chocolate and rinds in medium bowl. Add hot cream; stir until smooth. Cover bowl; refrigerate, stirring occasionally, about 30 minutes or until ganache is spreadable.

Grate the citrus rind called for here then save the fruit to extract the juice for another use. Without this protective 'skin', the fruit will become dry and hard, so they should be juiced, say for a salsa or salad dressing, within a day or two.

Date, ricotta & polenta cake

preparation time 30 minutes (plus standing time) **cooking time** 1 hour 55 minutes (plus cooling time) **serves** 16

1 cup (170g) finely chopped pitted dried dates

⅓ cup (80ml) orange-flavoured liqueur

2 cups (300g) self-raising flour

1 teaspoon baking powder

⅔ cup (110g) polenta

1 cup (220g) caster sugar

1¼ cups (250g) ricotta cheese

125g butter, melted

¾ cup (180ml) water

½ cup (75g) coarsely chopped roasted hazelnuts

ORANGE RICOTTA CREAM

1¼ cups (250g) ricotta cheese

2 tablespoons orange-flavoured liqueur

2 tablespoons icing sugar

1 tablespoon finely grated orange rind

1 Preheat oven to 160°C/140°C fan-assisted. Grease deep 22cm-round cake tin; line base and side with baking parchment.

2 Combine dates and liqueur in small bowl; stand 15 minutes.

3 Meanwhile, make orange ricotta cream.

4 Beat flour, baking powder, polenta, sugar, ricotta, butter and the water in large bowl on low speed with electric mixer until combined. Increase speed to medium; beat until mixture changes to a paler colour. Stir in nuts and undrained date mixture.

5 Spread half the cake mixture into tin; spread orange ricotta cream over cake mixture. Spread with remaining cake mixture.

6 Bake cake about 45 minutes. Cover tightly with foil; bake further 1 hour. Discard foil, stand cake in tin 10 minutes; turn, top-side up, onto wire rack to cool.

ORANGE RICOTTA CREAM Stir ingredients in medium bowl until smooth.

Raspberry hazelnut cake

preparation time 30 minutes **cooking time** 1 hour 30 minutes (plus cooling time) **serves** 12

250g butter, softened

2 cups (440g) caster sugar

6 eggs

1 cup (150g) plain flour

½ cup (75g) self-raising flour

1 cup (100g) ground hazelnuts

⅔ cup (160g) soured cream

300g fresh or frozen raspberries

¼ cup (35g) roasted hazelnuts, chopped coarsely

MASCARPONE CREAM

1 cup (250g) mascarpone cheese

¼ cup (40g) icing sugar

2 tablespoons hazelnut-flavoured liqueur

½ cup (120g) soured cream

1 Preheat oven to 180°C/160°C fan-assisted. Grease deep 22cm-round cake tin; line base and side with baking parchment.

2 Beat butter and sugar in medium bowl with electric mixer until light and fluffy. Beat in eggs, one at a time (mixture will curdle at this stage, but will come together later). Transfer mixture to large bowl; stir in sifted flours, hazelnut meal, soured cream and raspberries. Spread mixture into tin.

3 Bake cake about 1½ hours. Stand cake in tin 10 minutes; turn, top-side up, onto wire rack to cool.

4 Meanwhile, make mascarpone cream.

5 Spread mascarpone cream all over cold cake, top with nuts.

MASCARPONE CREAM Stir ingredients in medium bowl until smooth.

tips If using frozen raspberries, don't thaw them; frozen berries are less likely to 'bleed' into the cake mixture.

We used Frangelico, but you can use any hazelnut-flavoured liqueur.

55

Upside-down toffee date & banana cake

preparation time 20 minutes **cooking time** 1 hour 10 minutes **serves** 12

1½ cups (330g) caster sugar

1½ cups (375ml) water

3 star anise

2 medium bananas (400g), sliced thinly

1 cup (140g) pitted dried dates

¾ cup (180ml) water, extra

½ cup (125ml) dark rum

1 teaspoon bicarbonate of soda

60g butter, chopped

½ cup (110g) firmly packed brown sugar

2 eggs

2 teaspoons mixed spice

1 cup (150g) self-raising flour

½ cup mashed banana

300ml whipping cream

1   Preheat oven to 180°C/160°C fan-assisted. Grease deep 22cm-round cake tin; line base with baking parchment.

2   Stir caster sugar, the water and star anise in medium saucepan over low heat, without boiling, until sugar dissolves. Bring to the boil; boil syrup, uncovered, without stirring, about 5 minutes or until thickened slightly. Strain ½ cup of the syrup into small heatproof jug; reserve to flavour cream. Discard star anise.

3   To make toffee, continue boiling remaining syrup, uncovered, without stirring, about 10 minutes or until golden brown. Pour hot toffee into cake tin; top with sliced banana.

4   Place dates, the extra water and rum in small saucepan; bring to the boil, remove from heat. Stir in soda; stand 5 minutes. Process date mixture with butter and brown sugar until almost smooth. Add eggs, spice and flour; process until just combined. Stir in mashed banana. Pour mixture into tin.

5   Bake cake about 40 minutes. Turn cake, in tin, onto serving plate; stand 2 minutes. Remove tin then peel away baking parchment.

6   To make star anise cream, beat cream in small bowl with electric mixer until firm peaks form. Stir in reserved syrup.

7   Serve cake warm or at room temperature with star anise cream.

tip You need 1 large overripe banana (230g) for the mashed banana.

Star anise, the dried, star-shaped fruit of a small Asian tree, has a pungent liquorice/clove/cinnamon flavour. Used whole or ground, it is the main spice in Chinese five-spice. Use sparingly with pork or duck or in a fruit compote.

Small Cakes

Mini chocolate hazelnut cakes

preparation time 25 minutes **cooking time** 25 minutes **makes** 12

100g dark eating chocolate, chopped coarsely

¾ cup (180ml) water

100g butter, softened

1 cup (220g) firmly packed brown sugar

3 eggs

¼ cup (25g) cocoa powder

¾ cup (110g) self-raising flour

⅓ cup (35g) ground hazelnuts

WHIPPED HAZELNUT GANACHE

⅓ cup (80ml) whipping cream

180g milk eating chocolate, chopped finely

2 tablespoons hazelnut-flavoured liqueur

1 Preheat oven to 180°C/160°C fan-assisted. Grease 12 holes of 2 x ½-cup (125ml) muffin pans.

2 Make whipped hazelnut ganache.

3 Meanwhile, stir chocolate and the water in medium saucepan over low heat until smooth.

4 Beat butter and sugar in small bowl with electric mixer until light and fluffy. Beat in eggs, one at a time (mixture may curdle at this stage, but will come together later); transfer mixture to medium bowl. Stir in warm chocolate mixture, sifted cocoa and flour, and ground hazelnuts. Divide mixture among pans.

5 Bake cakes about 20 minutes. Stand cakes in pans 5 minutes; turn, top-sides up, onto wire rack to cool. Spread ganache over cakes.

   WHIPPED HAZELNUT GANACHE Stir cream and chocolate in small saucepan over low heat until smooth. Stir in liqueur; transfer mixture to small bowl. Cover; stand about 2 hours or until just firm. Beat ganache in small bowl with electric mixer until mixture changes to a pale brown colour.

Rock cakes

preparation time 15 minutes **cooking time** 15 minutes **makes** 18

2 cups (300g) self-raising flour

¼ teaspoon ground cinnamon

⅓ cup (75g) caster sugar

90g butter, chopped

1 cup (160g) sultanas

1 egg, beaten lightly

½ cup (125ml) milk

1 tablespoon caster sugar, extra

1 Preheat oven to 200°C/180°C fan-assisted. Grease oven trays.
2 Sift flour, cinnamon and sugar into medium bowl; rub in butter with fingertips. Stir in sultanas, egg and milk. Do not over-mix.
3 Drop rounded tablespoons of mixture about 5cm apart onto trays; sprinkle with extra sugar.
4 Bake cakes about 15 minutes; cool on trays.

VARIATIONS

cranberry & fig Substitute caster sugar with ⅓ cup firmly packed brown sugar. Omit sultanas; stir 1 cup coarsely chopped dried figs and ¼ cup dried cranberries into mixture before egg and milk are added.

pineapple, lime & coconut Omit sultanas; stir 1 cup coarsely chopped dried pineapple, ¼ cup toasted flaked coconut and 1 teaspoon finely grated lime rind into mixture before egg and milk are added.

Apricot & honey rock cakes

preparation time 20 minutes **cooking time** 15 minutes **makes** 15

1 cup (160g) wholemeal self-raising flour

1 cup (150g) white self-raising flour

¼ cup (55g) caster sugar

¼ teaspoon ground cinnamon

90g butter, chopped

½ cup (80g) finely chopped dried apricots

2 tablespoons sultanas

1 egg

2 tablespoons honey

⅓ cup (80ml) milk

1 Preheat oven to 200°C/180°C fan-assisted. Grease two oven trays.
2 Sift dry ingredients into large bowl; rub in butter. Stir in apricots and sultanas. Combine egg and honey in small bowl; stir into mixture with milk.
3 Drop tablespoonfuls of the mixture in rough heaps onto trays. Bake, uncovered, about 15 minutes. Cool on trays.

tips Dating back to Victorian times, these soft little fruit and spice cakes are perfect for a tea break.
Try 2 tablespoons orange marmalade as an alternative to honey and ½ cup quartered glacé cherries instead of apricots.
Rock cakes are cooked when they still feel soft in the oven. When they look firm, push one with your finger. If it moves easily on the tray, the cakes are cooked; they will become firmer on cooling.
Rock cakes can be stored in an airtight container for up to 2 days.

Easy cupcakes

preparation time 20 minutes **cooking time** 20 minutes **makes** 24 cupcakes

125g butter, softened

½ teaspoon vanilla extract

¾ cup (165g) caster sugar

3 eggs

2 cups (300g) self-raising flour

¼ cup (60ml) milk

1 Preheat oven to 180°C/160°C fan-assisted. Line two 12-hole muffin pans with paper cases.
2 Combine ingredients in medium bowl; beat with electric mixer on low speed until ingredients are just combined. Increase speed to medium; beat about 3 minutes or until mixture is smooth and paler in colour.
3 Drop rounded tablespoons of mixture into each case; bake about 20 minutes. Stand cakes 5 minutes; turn, top-sides up, onto wire racks to cool.
4 Top cakes with icing of your choice.

VARIATIONS

chocolate & orange Stir in 1 teaspoon finely grated orange rind and ½ cup (95g) dark chocolate chips at the end of step 2.
passionfruit & lime Stir in 1 teaspoon finely grated lime rind and ¼ cup (60ml) passionfruit pulp at the end of step 2.
banana & white chocolate chip Stir in ½ cup overripe mashed banana and ½ cup (95g) white chocolate chips at the end of step 2.
mocha Blend 1 tablespoon sifted cocoa powder with 1 tablespoon strong black coffee; stir in at the end of step 2.

Glacé icing

2 cups (320g) icing sugar

20g butter, melted

2 tablespoons hot water, approximately

1 Place sifted icing sugar in small bowl; stir in butter and enough of the hot water to make a firm paste; stir over small saucepan of simmering water until spreadable.

VARIATIONS

chocolate Stir in 1 teaspoon sifted cocoa powder.
coffee Dissolve 1 teaspoon instant coffee granules in the hot water.
passionfruit Stir in 1 tablespoon passionfruit pulp.

For easy butterfly cakes, use a sharp pointed vegetable knife to cut a small round cavity out of the centres of cupcakes. Cut the small pieces of cake in half to make the butterfly's wings. Fill the cavities of the cakes with jam and cream (or the fillings of your choice). Position the wings on the cream, then dust the cakes with a little sifted icing sugar.

Hummingbird cupcakes

preparation time 20 minutes **cooking time** 25 minutes **makes** 12

440g can crushed pineapple in syrup

1 cup (160g) wholemeal plain flour

½ cup (80g) wholemeal self-raising flour

½ teaspoon bicarbonate of soda

½ teaspoon ground cinnamon

½ teaspoon ground ginger

1 cup (220g) firmly packed brown sugar

2 eggs, beaten lightly

¼ cup (20g) desiccated coconut

¾ cup mashed banana

⅓ cup (80ml) vegetable oil

½ cup (80g) icing sugar

2 tablespoons toasted shredded coconut

1   Preheat oven to 180°C/160°C fan-assisted. Line 12-hole (⅓-cup/80ml) muffin pan with paper cases.

2   Drain pineapple over small bowl, pressing with spoon to extract as much syrup as possible. Reserve ⅓ cup of the syrup, discard remainder.

3   Sift flours, soda, spices and brown sugar into medium bowl. Stir in ¼ cup of the reserved syrup, egg, desiccated coconut, banana and oil. Divide mixture among paper cases.

4   Bake cupcakes about 25 minutes. Stand cakes in pan 5 minutes; turn, top-side up, onto wire rack to cool.

5   Meanwhile, place icing sugar in small bowl; add enough of the remaining syrup to make icing spreadable. Drizzle cupcakes with icing, sprinkle with shredded coconut.

tip You need 2 medium overripe bananas (460g) for this recipe.

Gluten-free berry cupcakes

preparation time 20 minutes **cooking time** 25 minutes **makes** 12

125g butter, softened

2 teaspoons finely grated lemon rind

¾ cup (165g) caster sugar

4 eggs

2 cups (240g) ground almonds

½ cup (40g) desiccated coconut

½ cup (100g) rice flour

1 teaspoon bicarbonate of soda

1 cup (150g) frozen mixed berries

1 tablespoon desiccated coconut, extra

1   Preheat oven to 180°C/160°C fan-assisted. Grease 12-hole (⅓-cup/80ml) muffin pan.

2   Beat butter, rind and sugar in small bowl with electric mixer until light and fluffy. Beat in eggs, one at a time (mixture may curdle at this stage, but will come together later). Transfer mixture to large bowl; stir in ground almonds, coconut, sifted flour and bicarbonate of soda, then berries. Divide mixture among pan holes.

3   Bake cupcakes about 25 minutes. Stand cupcakes in pan 5 minutes; turn, top-sides up, onto wire rack to cool. Sprinkle with extra desiccated coconut.

Carrot cupcakes with maple cream cheese frosting

preparation time 25 minutes (plus cooling time) **cooking time** 30 minutes **makes** 12

1½ cups (225g) self-raising flour

1 cup (220g) firmly packed brown sugar

2 teaspoons mixed spice

½ cup (125ml) vegetable oil

3 eggs

2 cups (480g) firmly packed coarsely grated carrot

¾ cup (90g) coarsely chopped roasted pecans

6 roasted pecans, halved

MAPLE CREAM CHEESE FROSTING

30g butter, softened

80g cream cheese, softened

2 tablespoons maple syrup

1¼ cups (200g) icing sugar

1   Preheat oven to 180°C/160°C fan-assisted. Line 12-hole (⅓-cup/80ml) muffin pan with paper cases.

2   Combine sifted flour, sugar, spice, oil and eggs in medium bowl. Stir in carrot and chopped nuts. Divide mixture among paper cases.

3   Bake cupcakes about 30 minutes. Stand cakes in pan 5 minutes; turn, top-side up, onto wire rack to cool.

4   Meanwhile, make maple cream cheese frosting.

5   Spread frosting over cupcakes; top each with a nut.
MAPLE CREAM CHEESE FROSTING Beat butter, cream cheese and syrup in small bowl with electric mixer until light and fluffy; gradually beat in sifted icing sugar until spreadable.

tip You will need about 4 medium carrots (480g) for this recipe.

Carrots are often used in cooking to add sweetness to dishes. It is believed that carrot cakes are an adaptation of carrot pudding, which was popular in the UK in the 18th and 19th centuries. Remember to use a light blended vegetable oil, such as corn, sunflower or canola, to allow the carrot flavour to shine through.

Coconut cupcakes

preparation time 20 minutes (plus cooling time) **cooking time** 30 minutes **makes** 12

125g unsalted butter, softened

1 teaspoon finely grated lemon rind

¾ cup (165g) caster sugar

2 eggs

½ cup (40g) desiccated coconut

1¼ cups (185g) self-raising flour

½ cup (125ml) milk

2 tablespoons desiccated coconut, extra

PINK GLACE ICING

1¼ cups (200g) icing sugar, sifted

1 tablespoon boiling water, approximately

pink food colouring

1 Preheat oven to 180°C/160°C fan-assisted. Line 12-hole (⅓-cup/80ml) muffin pan with paper cases.

2 Beat butter, rind and sugar in small bowl with electric mixer until light and fluffy. Beat in eggs, one at a time. Transfer mixture to large bowl; stir in desiccated coconut, sifted flour, and milk in two batches.

3 Divide mixture into paper cases; bake about 30 minutes. Stand cupcakes in pan 5 minutes before turning, top-side up, onto wire rack to cool.

4 Make pink glace icing. Spread icing over cold cupcakes; sprinkle with extra coconut.
PINK GLACE ICING Sift icing sugar into small bowl; stir in enough water to make icing spreadable. Tint pink with colouring.

Banana cupcakes with maple frosting

preparation time 10 minutes **cooking time** 30 minutes **makes** 12

60g butter, softened

60g soft cream cheese

¾ cup (165g) firmly packed brown sugar

2 eggs

½ cup (125ml) milk

2 tablespoons maple syrup

1½ cups (225g) self-raising flour

½ teaspoon bicarbonate of soda

2 medium bananas (400g), halved lengthways, sliced thinly

MAPLE FROSTING

30g butter, softened

80g soft cream cheese

2 tablespoons maple syrup

1½ cups (240g) icing sugar

1 Preheat oven to 180°C/160°C fan-assisted. Line 12-hole (⅓-cup/80ml) muffin pan with paper cases.

2 Beat butter, cream cheese and sugar in medium bowl with electric mixer until light and fluffy. Beat in eggs, one at a time. Stir in milk, syrup and sifted dry ingredients; fold in bananas.

3 Drop ¼ cups of mixture into each paper case; bake about 30 minutes. Stand cakes in pans 5 minutes before turning, top-side up, onto wire rack to cool.

4 Meanwhile, make maple cream frosting. Spread cakes with frosting.
MAPLE FROSTING Beat butter, cream cheese and syrup in small bowl with electric mixer until light and fluffy; beat in sifted icing sugar, in two batches, until combined.

Walnut brownie bites

preparation time 15 minutes (plus standing time) **cooking time** 20 minutes (plus cooling time) **makes** 24

½ cup (50g) walnuts, toasted, chopped finely

80g butter

150g dark chocolate, chopped coarsely

¾ cup (150g) firmly packed brown sugar

1 egg, beaten lightly

⅓ cup (50g) plain flour

¼ cup (60g) soured cream

3 x 50g packet Rolos™

1 Preheat oven to 180°C/160°C fan-assisted. Lightly grease two non-stick 12-hole 1½-tablespoon (30ml) mini muffin pans; divide walnuts among holes.

2 Stir butter and chocolate in small saucepan over low heat until smooth. Stir in sugar; cool to just warm.

3 Stir in egg, then flour and soured cream; spoon mixture into prepared pan. Press one Rolo™ into centre of each quantity of mixture; spread mixture so that Rolo™ is completely enclosed. Bake cakes 15 minutes. Using a sharp-pointed knife, loosen sides of brownies from pan; stand 10 minutes. Remove brownies gently from pan.

tip These little treats are best served while still warm.

Choc fudge cakes with coffee syrup

preparation time 15 minutes **cooking time** 20 minutes **makes** 12

½ cup (50g) cocoa powder

1 cup (220g) firmly packed brown sugar

½ cup (125ml) boiling water

85g dark cooking chocolate, chopped finely

2 egg yolks

¼ cup (30g) ground almonds

⅓ cup (50g) wholemeal plain flour

4 egg whites

COFFEE SYRUP

¾ cup (165g) firmly packed brown sugar

¾ cup (180ml) water

1 tablespoon instant coffee powder

1 Preheat oven to 170°C/150°C fan-assisted. Lightly grease 12-hole (⅓-cup/80ml) muffin pan.

2 Combine sifted cocoa and sugar in large bowl; blend in the water then chocolate, stir until smooth. Stir in egg yolks, ground almonds and flour.

3 Beat egg whites in small bowl with electric mixer until soft peaks form. Fold egg whites into chocolate mixture, in two batches; divide mixture among prepared holes of muffin pan. Bake, uncovered, about 20 minutes.

4 Meanwhile, make coffee syrup.

5 Stand cakes in pan 5 minutes, divide among plates; drizzle hot cakes with hot coffee syrup.

COFFEE SYRUP Stir sugar and the water in small saucepan over low heat until sugar dissolves; bring to a boil. Reduce heat; simmer, uncovered, without stirring, about 15 minutes or until syrup thickens. Stir in coffee; strain into small heatproof jug.

Rhubarb & almond cakes

preparation time 20 minutes **cooking time** 40 minutes **makes** 6

½ cup (125ml) milk

¼ cup (40g) blanched almonds, toasted

80g butter, softened

1 teaspoon vanilla extract

½ cup (110g) caster sugar

2 eggs

1 cup (150g) self-raising flour

POACHED RHUBARB

250g trimmed rhubarb, chopped coarsely

¼ cup (60ml) water

½ cup (110g) white sugar

1 Preheat oven to 180°C/160°C fan-assisted. Grease a 6-hole large (¾-cup/180ml) muffin pan.

2 Make poached rhubarb.

3 Meanwhile, blend or process milk and nuts until smooth.

4 Beat butter, extract and sugar in small bowl with electric mixer until light and fluffy. Add eggs, one at a time, beating until just combined between additions (mixture might separate at this stage, but will come together later); transfer to large bowl. Stir in sifted flour and almond mixture.

5 Spoon mixture equally among muffin pan holes; bake 10 minutes. Carefully remove muffin pan from oven; divide drained rhubarb over muffins, bake further 15 minutes.

6 Stand muffins 5 minutes; turn, top-side up, onto wire rack to cool. Serve warm or cold with rhubarb syrup.

POACHED RHUBARB Place ingredients in medium saucepan; bring to a boil. Reduce heat; simmer, uncovered, about 10 minutes or until rhubarb is just tender. Drain rhubarb over medium bowl; reserve rhubarb and syrup separately.

Thanks to hothouse growing, rhubarb is available all year, so you can indulge in a hot pie or crumble as well as any number of luscious cakes and desserts matching rhubarb with berries and cream or mascarpone whenever you like. Be sure to discard every bit of the vegetable's leaf and use only the thinnest stalks (the thick ones tend to be stringy).

Chocolate coconut cakes

preparation time 20 minutes **cooking time** 30 minutes **makes** 6

⅔ cup (150g) firmly packed brown sugar

¼ cup (25g) cocoa powder

½ cup (75g) self-raising flour

½ cup (75g) plain flour

⅓ cup (25g) desiccated coconut

125g butter, melted

1 egg

⅓ cup (80ml) milk

CHOCOLATE BUTTERCREAM

70g butter, softened

1 tablespoon milk

¾ cup (120g) icing sugar

2 tablespoons cocoa powder, sifted

1 Preheat oven to 160°C/140°C fan-assisted. Grease 6-hole large (¾-cup/180ml) muffin pan.

2 Sift sugar, cocoa and flours in medium bowl; stir in coconut, butter and combined egg and milk. Divide mixture among pan holes; bake about 35 minutes. Stand 5 minutes; turn onto wire rack to cool.

3 Make chocolate buttercream; spread over cold cakes.
CHOCOLATE BUTTERCREAM Beat ingredients in small bowl with electric mixer until light and fluffy.

Coffee caramel cakes

preparation time 15 minutes **cooking time** 20 minutes (plus cooling time) **makes** 12

125g butter, softened

⅔ cup (150g) firmly packed brown sugar

2 tablespoons instant coffee granules

1 tablespoon boiling water

2 eggs

2 cups (300g) self-raising flour

½ cup (125ml) milk

18 (130g) soft caramels, halved

1 Preheat oven to 180°C/160°C fan-assisted. Grease 12-hole (⅓-cup/80ml) muffin pan.

2 Beat butter and sugar in small bowl with electric mixer until light and fluffy. Add combined coffee and the water; beat in eggs, one at a time. Transfer mixture to large bowl; stir in sifted flour and milk.

3 Spoon mixture into pan holes. Press 3 caramel halves into the centre of each cake; cover with mixture.

4 Bake cakes about 20 minutes. Stand cakes in pan 5 minutes; turn, top-side up, onto wire racks to cool.

tips These cakes are best made on day of serving. Cakes suitable to freeze for up to 1 month.

Ginger cakes with orange glaze

preparation time 15 minutes **cooking time** 30 minutes (plus standing time) **makes** 8

⅔ cup (100g) plain flour

⅔ cup (100g) self-raising flour

½ teaspoon bicarbonate of soda

2 teaspoons ground cinnamon

2 teaspoons ground ginger

½ teaspoon ground cloves

1 cup (220g) firmly packed brown sugar

⅔ cup (160ml) buttermilk

2 eggs, beaten lightly

100g unsalted butter, melted

ORANGE GLAZE

1 cup (160g) icing sugar

½ teaspoon finely grated orange rind

1 tablespoon strained orange juice

2 teaspoons hot water

1 Preheat oven to 180°C/160°C fan-assisted. Grease and flour 8 holes of two 6-hole (¾-cup/180ml) mini fluted tube pans.

2 Sift flours, soda, spices and sugar into medium bowl, add buttermilk, egg and butter; stir until smooth. Divide mixture among pan holes; bake about 30 minutes.

3 Turn cakes immediately onto greased wire rack placed over tray. Allow to cool.

4 Make orange glaze.

5 Pour glaze over cakes; stand until glaze is set.
   ORANGE GLAZE Sift icing sugar into medium bowl, add remaining ingredients; stir until smooth.

Cake tins are available in many different shapes and sizes and made from a range of materials. We tested these recipes using aluminium cake tins. Pans made from tin or stainless steel do not conduct heat as evenly as aluminium. Cake tins with a non-stick coating work well provided the surface is unscratched. These ginger cakes work just as well cooked in muffin pans.

small cakes

Little lime syrup cakes

preparation time 10 minutes **cooking time** 25 minutes **makes** 6

125g butter, chopped

½ cup (110g) caster sugar

2 teaspoons grated lime rind

2 eggs

1 cup (150g) self-raising flour

½ cup (125ml) buttermilk

LIME SYRUP

⅓ cup (80ml) lime juice

½ cup (110g) caster sugar

2 tablespoons water

1 teaspoon grated lime rind

1 Preheat oven to 180ºC/160ºC fan-assisted. Grease a six-hole mini fluted tube pan or large (¾-cup/180ml) muffin pan.
2 Beat butter, sugar and rind in small bowl with electric mixer until light and fluffy. Add eggs, one at a time, beating until just combined between additions.
3 Transfer mixture to medium bowl; stir in sifted flour and buttermilk.
4 Divide mixture among prepared holes, smooth tops. Bake cakes about 25 minutes.
5 Meanwhile, make lime syrup.
6 Stand cakes 5 minutes before turning onto wire rack over a tray. Pour hot lime syrup evenly over hot cakes. Serve cakes warm or cooled with whipped cream, if desired.
   LIME SYRUP Combine all ingredients except grated lime rind in small saucepan; stir over low heat until sugar dissolved. Bring to a boil; remove from heat. Stir in grated lime rind.

Apple ginger cakes with lemon icing

preparation time 15 minutes **cooking time** 25 minutes (plus cooling time) **makes** 12

250g butter, softened

1½ cups (330g) firmly packed dark brown sugar

3 eggs

¼ cup (90g) golden syrup

2 cups (300g) plain flour

1½ teaspoons bicarbonate of soda

2 tablespoons ground ginger

1 tablespoon ground cinnamon

1 cup (170g) coarsely grated apple

⅔ cup (160ml) hot water

LEMON ICING

2 cups (320g) icing sugar

2 teaspoons butter, softened

⅓ cup (80ml) lemon juice

1 Preheat oven to 180ºC/160ºC fan-assisted. Grease two 6-hole mini fluted tube pans.
2 Beat butter and sugar in small bowl with electric mixer until light and fluffy. Beat in eggs, one at a time. Stir in syrup. Transfer mixture to medium bowl; stir in sifted dry ingredients, then apple and the water. Divide mixture among pans; smooth surface.
3 Bake cakes about 25 minutes. Stand cakes in pan 5 minutes; turn, top-side down, onto wire racks to cool.
4 Meanwhile, make lemon icing; drizzle icing over warm cakes.
   LEMON ICING Sift icing sugar into small heatproof bowl; stir in butter and juice to form a paste. Place bowl over small saucepan of simmering water; stir until icing is a pouring consistency.

tips You can also make these cakes in 6-hole texas (¾-cup/180ml) muffin pans lined with paper cases.
These cakes can be stored in an airtight container for up to 3 days.
Un-iced cakes can be frozen for up to 3 months.
You need 1 large apple (200g) for this recipe.

Almond friands

preparation time 20 minutes   **cooking time** 25 minutes   **makes** 12

6 egg whites

185g butter, melted

1 cup (120g) ground almonds

1½ cups (240g) icing sugar

½ cup (75g) plain flour

1 Preheat oven to 200°C/180°C fan-assisted. Grease 12 x ½ cup (125ml) friand or muffin pans; place on oven tray.
2 Place egg whites in medium bowl; beat with a fork. Stir in butter, ground almonds and sifted icing sugar and flour until just combined.
3 Spoon mixture into pans.
4 Bake friands about 25 minutes. Stand in pans 5 minutes before turning, top-side up, onto wire rack. Serve dusted with extra sifted icing sugar, if you like.

VARIATIONS

raspberry & white chocolate Stir 100g coarsely chopped white chocolate into egg-white mixture. Top friands with 100g fresh or frozen raspberries.

lime coconut Stir 2 teaspoons finely grated lime rind, 1 tablespoon lime juice and ¼ cup (20g) desiccated coconut into egg-white mixture; sprinkle unbaked friands with ⅓ cup (15g) flaked coconut.

passionfruit Use either ground almonds or hazelnuts, then drizzle the pulp of 2 medium passionfruit over unbaked friands.

berry Top unbaked friands with 100g fresh or frozen mixed berries.

citrus & poppy seed Add 2 teaspoons grated lemon or orange rind and 1 tablespoon poppy seeds to egg-white mixture.

chocolate & hazelnut Replace ground almonds with ground hazelnuts. Stir 100g coarsely chopped dark chocolate into egg-white mixture. Sprinkle unbaked friands with ¼ cup coarsely chopped hazelnuts.

plum Use ground hazelnuts or almonds. Top unbaked friands with 2 medium (200g) thinly sliced plums.

tips Friands are best made on the day of serving, but can be stored in an airtight container for 2 days, or frozen for up to 3 months.
If you can't find the traditional oval friand pans, deep muffin pans will serve just as well.

Friands are small densely-textured little sponge cakes, popular in Australia and New Zealand and similar to French Financiers. Traditionally baked in oval shapes, they gain their texture from the icing sugar and ground almonds that partly replaces the flour and they come in a variety of flavourings.

ond

raspberry & white chocolate

lime coconut

ssionfruit

citrus & poppy seed

chocolate & hazelnut

Glacé fruit cakes with ginger syrup

preparation time 25 minutes **cooking time** 25 minutes **makes** 12

¾ cup (105g) slivered almonds

90g butter, softened

2 teaspoons finely grated lemon rind

¾ cup (165g) caster sugar

2 eggs

¾ cup (110g) plain flour

½ cup (75g) self-raising flour

⅓ cup (80ml) milk

4 slices glacé pineapple (125g), chopped coarsely

⅓ cup (70g) red glacé cherries, halved

⅓ cup (70g) green glacé cherries, halved

⅓ cup (75g) coarsely chopped stem ginger

½ cup (70g) slivered almonds, extra

GINGER SYRUP

¾ cup (180ml) water

¾ cup (165g) caster sugar

2cm piece fresh ginger (10g), grated

1 Preheat oven to 170°C/150°C fan-assisted. Grease 12-hole (⅓-cup/80ml) muffin pan; line bases with baking parchment.
2 Sprinkle nuts into pan holes.
3 Beat butter, rind and sugar in small bowl with electric mixer until light and fluffy. Beat in eggs one at a time.
4 Transfer mixture to medium bowl; stir in sifted flours, milk, fruit and extra nuts. Spread mixture into pan holes.
5 Bake cakes about 25 minutes.
6 Meanwhile, make ginger syrup.
7 Remove cakes from oven; pour hot syrup over hot cakes in pan. Cool cakes in pan.
8 Serve cakes warm or cold with cream or ice-cream.
   GINGER SYRUP Stir ingredients in small saucepan over heat, without boiling, until sugar dissolves; bring to the boil. Reduce heat; simmer, uncovered, without stirring, about 5 minutes or until syrup thickens slightly.

Stem ginger is fresh ginger root preserved in a sugar syrup; it has a smooth, rich ginger flavour with an added hint of subtle heat. It can be eaten as a snack as well as (by far its most common use) used to add a flavourful burst of ginger when baking. Crystallised ginger can be substituted if rinsed with warm water and dried before using.

Orange blossom cakes

preparation time 20 minutes **cooking time** 25 minutes **makes** 6

100g butter, softened

1 teaspoon orange flower water

½ cup (110g) caster sugar

2 eggs

1 cup (150g) self-raising flour

¼ cup (30g) ground almonds

½ cup (125ml) milk

ORANGE BLOSSOM GLACÉ ICING

1 cup (160g) icing sugar

10g softened butter

1 teaspoon orange flower water

1 tablespoon water, approximately

1 Preheat oven to 180ºC/160ºC fan-assisted. Grease six-hole (¾-cup/180ml) mini fluted tube pan or large muffin pan.

2 Beat butter, flower water and sugar in small bowl with electric mixer until light and fluffy. Beat in eggs, one at a time (mixture will curdle). Stir in sifted flour, almonds and milk, in two batches.

3 Divide mixture into pan holes; bake about 25 minutes. Stand cakes in pan 5 minutes before turning, top-side up, onto wire rack to cool.

4 Meanwhile, make orange blossom glacé icing. Drizzle over cakes.
ORANGE BLOSSOM GLACÉ ICING Sift icing sugar into small heatproof bowl; stir in butter, flower water and enough of the boiling water to make a firm paste. Stir over small saucepan of simmering water until icing is pourable.

tip Orange flower water is a concentrated flavouring made from orange blossoms; it is available from Middle-Eastern food stores, some supermarkets and delicatessens. Citrus flavourings are very different.

Orange syrup cakes

preparation time 25 minutes **cooking time** 1 hour 10 minutes (plus cooling time) **makes** 24

3 medium oranges (720g)

250g butter, chopped coarsely

1½ cups (330g) caster sugar

4 eggs

¾ cup (120g) semolina

¾ cup (90g) ground almonds

¾ cup (110g) self-raising flour

ORANGE SYRUP

1 medium orange (240g)

½ cup (110g) caster sugar

1 cup (250ml) water

1 Preheat oven to 160°C/140°C fan-assisted. Line two 12-hole (⅓-cup/80ml) muffin pans with paper cases.

2 Coarsely chop oranges, including skin; remove and discard seeds. Place oranges in medium saucepan, add enough boiling water to cover. Bring to the boil, simmer, uncovered, about 15 minutes or until tender; cool. Drain oranges, then blend or process until smooth.

3 Beat butter and sugar in small bowl with electric mixer until light and fluffy. Beat in eggs, one at a time. Transfer mixture to large bowl; stir in semolina, ground almonds and sifted flour, then orange purée. Spoon mixture into paper cases. Bake cakes about 40 minutes.

5 Meanwhile, make orange syrup. Place hot cakes on wire rack over oven tray. Pour hot syrup over hot cakes. Serve warm or cold.
ORANGE SYRUP Peel rind thinly from orange, avoiding any white pith. Cut rind into thin strips. Stir sugar and the water in small saucepan over low heat, without boiling, until sugar is dissolved. Bring syrup to the boil; add rind, simmer, uncovered, 5 minutes. Transfer syrup to a heatproof jug.

tip These cakes can be made 4 days ahead. Not suitable to freeze.

Berry muffins

preparation time 10 minutes **cooking time** 20 minutes **makes** 12

2½ cups (375g) self-raising flour

90g cold butter, chopped

1 cup (220g) caster sugar

1¼ cups (310ml) buttermilk

1 egg, beaten lightly

200g fresh or frozen mixed berries

1 Preheat oven to 180°C/160°C fan-assisted. Grease 12-hole (⅓-cup/80ml) muffin pan.

2 Sift flour into large bowl; rub in butter. Stir in sugar, buttermilk and egg. Do not over-mix; mixture should be lumpy. Add berries; stir through gently.

3 Spoon mixture into pan holes; bake about 20 minutes. Stand muffins 5 minutes; turn, top-side up, onto wire rack to cool.

tip Muffins can be stored in an airtight container for up to 2 days.

VARIATIONS

lemon poppy seed Omit berries. Add 2 teaspoons lemon rind and 2 tablespoons poppy seeds with the sugar.

date & orange Omit berries. Substitute self-raising flour with 1 cup wholemeal self-raising flour and 1½ cups white self-raising flour. Add 1½ cups pitted, chopped dried dates and 2 teaspoons finely grated orange rind with the sugar.

choc chip & walnut Omit mixed berries. Add ¾ cup dark chocolate chips and 1 cup coarsely chopped walnuts with the sugar.

You can use any berries you like in this recipe – raspberries, blueberries and blackberries all work well – or you can use a mixture. If using frozen berries, use them straight from the freezer as thawed berries will bleed colour through the cake mixture.

Chocolate fudge mud cakes

preparation time 20 minutes **cooking time** 25 minutes **makes** 12

3 x 60g Mars Bars™

150g butter, chopped coarsely

150g dark eating chocolate, chopped coarsely

½ cup (110g) firmly packed brown sugar

1 cup (250ml) water

½ cup (75g) plain flour

¼ cup (35g) self-raising flour

2 eggs

CHOCOLATE FUDGE FROSTING

50g dark eating chocolate, chopped coarsely

25g butter

1 cup (160g) icing sugar

1 tablespoon cocoa powder

2 tablespoons hot water, approximately

1 Preheat oven to 180ºC/160ºC fan-assisted. Grease 12-hole (⅓-cup/80ml) muffin pan.

2 Chop two Mars Bars™ finely; cut remaining bar into 12 slices.

3 Combine butter, chocolate, sugar and the water in medium saucepan; stir over low heat until smooth. Transfer to large bowl; cool 10 minutes. Whisk in sifted flours then eggs and finely chopped Mars Bars™.

4 Divide mixture into pan holes; bake about 25 minutes. Stand cakes in pan 5 minutes before turning, top-side up, onto wire rack to cool.

5 Meanwhile, make chocolate fudge frosting. Spread cakes with frosting; top each with a slice of Mars Bar™.
   CHOCOLATE FUDGE FROSTING Stir chocolate and butter in small heatproof bowl over small saucepan of simmering water until smooth (do not allow water to touch base of bowl); stir in sifted icing sugar and cocoa. Stir in enough of the hot water until frosting is spreadable.

Chocolate sticky date cakes

preparation time 20 minutes **cooking time** 25 minutes **makes** 16

1¾ cups (250g) pitted dried dates

1⅓ cups (330ml) boiling water

1 teaspoon bicarbonate of soda

125g butter, softened

¾ cup (165g) firmly packed brown sugar

3 eggs

1½ cups (225g) self-raising flour

½ cup (95g) dark chocolate chips

CHOCOLATE ICING

1½ cups (240g) icing sugar

1 tablespoon cocoa powder

50g butter, melted

2 tablespoons hot water, approximately

1 Preheat oven to 180ºC/160ºC fan-assisted. Grease 16 holes of two 12-hole (⅓-cup/80ml) muffin pans.

2 Combine dates and the water in small saucepan; bring to the boil. Remove from heat; stir in bicarbonate of soda, stand 10 minutes. Blend or process mixture until almost smooth. Cool 10 minutes.

3 Beat butter and sugar in small bowl with electric mixer until light and fluffy. Beat in eggs, one at a time. Transfer mixture to large bowl; stir in sifted flour, chocolate and date mixture.

4 Divide mixture into pan holes; bake about 25 minutes. Stand cakes in pan 10 minutes before turning, top-side up, onto wire rack to cool.

5 Meanwhile, make chocolate icing. Spread cakes with icing.
   CHOCOLATE ICING Sift icing sugar and cocoa into small bowl; stir in butter and enough hot water to make icing spreadable.

Loaf Cakes

Cherry syrup loaf

preparation time 20 minutes (plus cooling time) **cooking time** 1 hour **serves** 8

125g unsalted butter, softened

1 teaspoon finely grated lemon rind

¾ cup (165g) caster sugar

2 eggs

1¾ cups (260g) self-raising flour

¾ cup (180ml) buttermilk

CHERRY SYRUP

1 cup (220g) caster sugar

2 tablespoons lemon juice

½ cup (125ml) water

680g jar morello cherries, drained

1 Preheat oven to 170°C/150°C fan-assisted. Grease 8cm x 20cm (5-cup/1.25-litre) loaf tin; line base and long sides with baking parchment, extending paper 5cm over sides.

2 Beat butter, rind and sugar in small bowl with electric mixer until light and fluffy. Beat in eggs, one at a time. Transfer mixture to large bowl; stir in sifted flour and buttermilk, in two batches.

3 Spread mixture into tin; bake about 1 hour. Stand cake in tin 5 minutes before turning, top-side up, onto wire rack placed over oven tray; remove baking parchment. Cool.

4 Meanwhile, make cherry syrup.

5 Slowly spoon hot syrup and cherries over cake. Place cake on plate; pour syrup from tray into jug.

6 Serve cake slices drizzled with remaining syrup.

CHERRY SYRUP Combine sugar, juice and the water in medium saucepan. Stir over heat, without boiling, until sugar dissolves; bring to the boil. Boil, uncovered, without stirring, 2 minutes. Add cherries, bring to the boil; reduce heat, simmer 2 minutes.

Apricot loaf

preparation time 15 minutes **cooking time** 1 hour 25 minutes (plus cooling time) **serves** 8

200g dried apricots, chopped coarsely

½ cup (125ml) apricot nectar

½ cup (110g) caster sugar

½ cup (110g) firmly packed brown sugar

250g butter, chopped

3 eggs

1 cup (150g) plain flour

¾ cup (110g) self-raising flour

1 Preheat oven to 150°C/130°C fan-assisted. Grease 14cm x 21cm loaf tin; line base and long sides with baking parchment, extending paper 2cm over sides.

2 Bring apricots, nectar and sugars to the boil in medium saucepan. reduce heat; simmer, covered, 5 minutes, stirring occasionally. Remove from heat; add butter, stir until melted. Transfer mixture to large bowl; cover, cool to room temperature.

3 Stir eggs and sifted flours into apricot mixture. Spread mixture into tin.

4 Bake loaf about 1¼ hours. Cover loaf with foil; cool in tin.

tips This loaf can be stored, covered, in an airtight container for up to 2 days or frozen for up to 3 months.

Apricot nectar is a sweetened purée of apricots, available in cans or bottles. If you can't get hold of it, buy a can of apricots in syrup and pass them through a sieve or blender to obtain a thick purée.

Sweet potato & pecan loaf

preparation time 20 minutes **cooking time** 1 hour 40 minutes **serves** 10

200g butter, softened

¾ cup (165g) firmly packed brown sugar

2 eggs

¾ cup (90g) pecans, chopped coarsely

½ cup (40g) desiccated coconut

1 cup mashed sweet potato

1½ cups (225g) self-raising flour

½ cup (125ml) milk

1 Preheat oven to 170°C/150°C fan-assisted. Grease 14cm x 21cm loaf tin; line base and long sides with baking parchment, extending paper 2cm over sides.

2 Beat butter, sugar and eggs in small bowl with electric mixer until just combined; transfer mixture to large bowl. Fold in nuts, coconut and sweet potato. Stir in sifted flour and milk, in two batches.

3 Spread mixture into tin; bake about 1 hour 40 minutes. Stand loaf 10 minutes; turn, top-side up, onto wire rack to cool.

Date & maple loaf

preparation time 20 minutes **cooking time** 50 minutes **serves** 12

¾ cup (110g) finely chopped pitted dates

⅓ cup (80ml) boiling water

½ teaspoon bicarbonate of soda

¼ cup (90g) maple syrup

90g butter, softened

⅓ cup (75g) firmly packed brown sugar

2 eggs

¾ cup (120g) wholemeal self-raising flour

½ cup (75g) plain flour

MAPLE BUTTER

125g butter, softened

2 tablespoons maple syrup

1 Preheat oven to 180°C/160°C fan-assisted. Grease 14cm x 21cm loaf tin.

2 Combine dates and the water in small heatproof bowl. Stir in bicarbonate of soda; stand 5 minutes. Stir in maple syrup.

3 Meanwhile, beat butter and sugar in medium bowl with electric mixer until light and fluffy. Add eggs, one at a time, beating until just combined between additions (mixture will separate at this stage, but will come together later). Add butter mixture to date mixture; stir in sifted flours, in two batches.

4 Spread mixture into tin; bake about 50 minutes. Stand loaf in tin 10 minutes; turn, top-side up, onto wire rack to cool.

5 Meanwhile, make maple butter. Serve loaf either warm or cold with maple butter.

MAPLE BUTTER Whisk ingredients for maple butter in small bowl until combined.

Just as you do when making a traditional sticky date pudding, soften the dates by standing them for several minutes in bicarbonate of soda dissolved in boiling water. For the most flavourful results, always use pure maple syrup rather than maple-flavoured syrup when making this recipe.

Gingerbread loaves

preparation time 35 minutes **cooking time** 25 minutes (plus cooling time) **makes** 16

200g butter, softened

1¼ cups (275g) caster sugar

¾ cup (270g) treacle

2 eggs

3 cups (450g) plain flour

1½ tablespoons ground ginger

3 teaspoons mixed spice

1 teaspoon bicarbonate of soda

¾ cup (180ml) milk

VANILLA ICING

3 cups (500g) icing sugar

2 teaspoons butter, softened

½ teaspoon vanilla extract

⅓ cup (80ml) milk

1 Preheat oven to 180°C/160°C fan-assisted. Grease two 8-hole (½-cup/125ml) mini loaf pans.

2 Beat butter and sugar in small bowl with electric mixer until light and fluffy. Add treacle, beat 3 minutes. Beat in eggs, one at a time. Transfer mixture to large bowl; stir in sifted dry ingredients, then milk, in two batches. Divide mixture between pans.

3 Bake loaves about 25 minutes. Stand loaves in pans 5 minutes; turn, top-side up, onto wire rack to cool.

4 Meanwhile, make vanilla icing; spread over loaves.
VANILLA ICING Sift icing sugar into heatproof bowl; stir in butter, extract and milk to form a smooth paste. Place bowl over simmering water; stir until spreadable.

tips You could also bake this recipe in two 12-hole (⅓-cup/80ml) muffin pans; line 22 holes with paper cases.
These cakes can be stored in an airtight container for up to 4 days.
Un-iced cakes can be frozen for up to 3 months.

Pistachio & hazelnut loaves

preparation time 20 minutes **cooking time** 30 minutes **makes** 8

6 egg whites

185g butter, melted

¾ cup (75g) ground hazelnuts

¼ cup (35g) roasted shelled pistachios, chopped coarsely

1½ cups (240g) icing sugar

½ cup (75g) plain flour

2 teaspoons rosewater

⅓ cup (50g) roasted shelled pistachios, extra

TOFFEE SHARDS

⅔ cup (160ml) water

1⅓ cups (300g) caster sugar

1 Make toffee shards.

2 Preheat oven to 200°C/180°C fan-assisted. Grease 8 x ½ cup (125ml) mini loaf tins; place on oven tray.

3 Place egg whites in medium bowl; beat with a fork. Stir in butter, ground hazelnuts, nuts, sugar, flour and rosewater until just combined. Spoon mixture into tins; top with extra nuts.

4 Bake loaves about 30 minutes. Stand in tins 5 minutes before turning, top-side up, onto wire rack.

5 Meanwhile, make toffee shards.

6 Serve loaves warm or at room temperature with toffee shards and thick cream, if you like.
TOFFEE SHARDS Stir ingredients in small saucepan over heat, without boiling, until sugar dissolves; bring to the boil. Reduce heat; simmer, uncovered, without stirring, about 10 minutes or until toffee is golden brown. Remove from heat; allow bubbles to subside. Pour hot toffee onto lightly oiled oven tray; do not scrape the toffee from pan, or it might crystallise. Allow toffee to set at room temperature; break into shards with hands.

Chocolate rum & raisin loaf

preparation time 20 minutes (plus standing time) **cooking time** 45 minutes **serves** 12

¾ cup (125g) raisins, chopped finely

¼ cup (60ml) dark rum

½ cup (110g) caster sugar

1 egg

1 teaspoon vanilla extract

2 tablespoons golden syrup

80g butter, melted

¾ cup (180ml) buttermilk

1 cup (150g) self-raising flour

2 tablespoons cocoa powder

¼ teaspoon ground nutmeg

⅓ cup (65g) dark chocolate chips, chopped coarsely

1 Preheat oven to 180°C/160°C fan-assisted. Lightly grease 14cm x 21cm loaf tin; line base and two long sides with baking parchment, extending paper 5cm above edges of tin.

2 Combine raisins and rum in small bowl; stand, covered, 2 hours.

3 Beat sugar, egg, extract and syrup in small bowl with electric mixer until thick and creamy.

4 Transfer mixture to medium bowl; stir in butter, buttermilk and sifted flour, cocoa and nutmeg. Stir in undrained raisin mixture and chocolate chips.

5 Spread mixture into prepared tin; bake, uncovered, about 45 minutes. Stand 10 minutes; turn onto wire rack to cool.

Banana bread

preparation time 10 minutes **cooking time** 30 minutes **serves** 12

1¼ cups (185g) self-raising flour

1 teaspoon ground cinnamon

20g butter

½ cup (100g) firmly packed brown sugar

1 egg, beaten lightly

¼ cup (60ml) milk

½ cup mashed banana

1 Preheat oven to 220°C/200°C fan-assisted. Grease 14cm x 21cm loaf tin; line base with baking parchment.

2 Sift flour and cinnamon into large bowl; rub in butter.

3 Stir in sugar, egg, milk and banana. Do not overmix, the batter should be lumpy. Spoon mixture into prepared tin. Bake loaf about 30 minutes or until cooked when tested; cool.

4 Cut bread into 12 slices; toast lightly. Spread each with a tablespoon of cream cheese and drizzle with a teaspoon of honey, if desired.

tips You will need 1 large (230g) banana for this recipe.
Bread can be made a day ahead and is also suitable to freeze.

Yogurt fruit loaf

preparation time 20 minutes **cooking time** 1 hour 30 minutes **serves** 12

100g butter, softened

2 teaspoons finely grated orange rind

¾ cup (165g) caster sugar

2 eggs

2 cups (320g) wholemeal self-raising flour

1 cup (280g) plain yogurt

⅓ cup (80ml) orange juice

1 cup (200g) finely chopped dried figs

1 cup (150g) coarsely chopped raisins

1 Preheat oven to 180°C/160°C fan-assisted. Grease 14cm x 21cm loaf tin.

2 Beat butter, rind, sugar, eggs, flour, yogurt and juice in medium bowl with electric mixer, on low speed, until just combined. Stir in fruit.

3 Pour mixture into tin; cover with foil. Bake 1 hour 15 minutes; remove foil, bake about a further 15 minutes. Stand loaf 10 minutes; turn, top-side up, onto wire rack to cool. Serve at room temperature or toasted, with butter.

Make a long, fairly wide pleat in the foil covering the tin to allow the fruit loaf to expand during baking. Use a full cream plain yogurt and not a light or low-fat variation in the mixture to ensure the quality of the finished product.

Cherry almond loaves

preparation time 15 minutes   **cooking time** 25 minutes   **makes** 12

6 egg whites

185g butter, melted

1 cup (125g) ground almonds

1½ cups (240g) icing sugar

½ cup (75g) plain flour

250g fresh cherries, halved, pitted

1 Preheat oven to 200°C/180°C fan-assisted. Grease 12 x ½ cup (125ml) mini loaf tins; stand tins on oven tray.

2 Place egg whites in medium bowl; beat with a fork. Stir in butter, ground almonds and sifted icing sugar and flour until just combined. Spoon mixture into tins; top with cherries.

3 Bake loaves about 25 minutes. Stand in tins 5 minutes before turning, top-side up, onto wire rack.

tips Cherries can be frozen for up to 18 months. Freeze them, in 250g batches, when they are in season.

If you use frozen cherries, be sure to use them unthawed – this will minimise the 'bleeding' of colour into the mixture.

Buttery apple cinnamon loaves

preparation time 10 minutes   **cooking time** 25 minutes (plus cooling time)   **makes** 8

125g butter, softened

1 teaspoon vanilla extract

¾ cup (165g) caster sugar

2 eggs

¾ cup (110g) self-raising flour

¼ cup (35g) plain flour

⅓ cup (80ml) apple juice

1 small red apple (130g)

1½ tablespoons demerara sugar

¼ teaspoon ground cinnamon

1 Preheat oven to 180°C/160°C fan-assisted. Grease 8-hole (½-cup/125ml) mini loaf pan.

2 Beat butter, extract and caster sugar in small bowl with electric mixer until light and fluffy. Beat in eggs, one at a time. Transfer mixture to medium bowl; fold in combined sifted flours and juice, in two batches. Spread mixture into pan holes.

3 Cut the unpeeled apple into quarters; remove core, slice thinly. Overlap apple slices on top of cakes.

4 Combine demerara sugar and cinnamon in small bowl; sprinkle half the sugar mixture over cakes.

5 Bake cakes about 25 minutes. Turn cakes, top-side up, onto wire rack to cool. Sprinkle with remaining sugar mixture.

tips These cakes can be stored in airtight container for up to 3 days or frozen for up to 3 months.

The cake mixture can also be cooked in a large muffin pan.

loaf cakes

Pineapple sultana loaf

preparation time 15 minutes cooking time 55 minutes serves 8

440g can crushed pineapple in juice, drained

1 cup (150g) self-raising flour

½ cup (110g) caster sugar

1 cup (80g) desiccated coconut

1 cup (160g) sultanas

1 egg, beaten lightly

½ cup (125ml) milk

1 Preheat oven to 180°C/160°C fan-assisted. Grease 14cm x 21cm loaf tin; line base with baking parchment, extending paper 5cm above long sides of tin.
2 Combine ingredients in large bowl. Pour mixture into tin; bake about 50 minutes. Stand loaf in tin 10 minutes; turn, top-side up, onto wire rack to cool.

Chocolate banana bread

preparation time 15 minutes cooking time 1 hour serves 12

1 cup mashed over-ripe banana

¾ cup (165g) caster sugar

2 eggs, beaten lightly

¼ cup (60ml) extra light olive oil

¼ cup (60ml) milk

⅔ cup (100g) self-raising flour

⅔ cup(100g) wholemeal self-raising flour

¾ cup (90g) coarsely chopped toasted walnuts

45g dark eating chocolate, finely chopped

WHIPPED NUT BUTTER

100g butter

¼ cup (30g) finely chopped toasted walnuts

1 Preheat oven to 180°C/160°C fan-assisted. Grease 14cm x 21cm loaf tin; line base and long sides with baking parchment.
2 Combine banana and sugar in large bowl; stir in eggs, oil and milk. Add flours, nuts and chocolate; stir until combined.
3 Spread mixture into prepared tin; bake, uncovered, about 1 hour. Stand bread in tin 5 minutes; turn onto wire rack to cool.
4 Make whipped nut butter. Serve bread warm with whipped nut butter.
   WHIPPED NUT BUTTER Beat butter in small bowl with electric mixer until light and fluffy; stir in nuts.

tips You will need 2 large (460g) bananas for this recipe. Leftover banana bread can be toasted if desired.

Wholemeal banana & prune bread

preparation time 15 minutes **cooking time** 1 hour **serves** 10

1½ cups (240g) wholemeal self-raising flour

1 teaspoon ground cinnamon

2 teaspoons finely grated lemon rind

100g butter, softened

¾ cup (165g) firmly packed dark brown sugar

2 eggs

1½ cups mashed banana

1 cup (170g) pitted prunes, chopped coarsely

1 Preheat oven to 180°C/160°C fan-assisted. Grease 14cm x 21cm loaf tin; line base and long sides with baking parchment, extending paper 2cm over sides.

2 Sift flour and cinnamon into large bowl; add rind, butter, sugar and eggs. Beat with electric mixer on low speed until ingredients are combined. Increase speed to medium; beat mixture until smooth. Stir in banana and prunes. Spread mixture into tin.

3 Bake bread about 1 hour. Stand bread in tin 5 minutes; turn, top-side up, onto wire rack to cool.

Make sure that the bananas you choose to mash for the cake mixture are over-ripe; if they are under-ripe, they won't mash easily and may cause the cake to be too heavy. You will need 3 large bananas (690g) for this recipe. Prunes are commercially or sun-dried plums; store them in the fridge.

Coffee walnut loaf

preparation time 25 minutes   **cooking time** 45 minutes   **serves** 10

⅔ cup (70g) roasted walnuts

125g butter, chopped

1 cup (220g) caster sugar

½ cup (125ml) milk

2 tablespoons instant coffee granules

1⅓ cups (200g) self-raising flour

2 teaspoons ground cinnamon

2 eggs, beaten lightly

COFFEE ICING

1 tablespoon boiling water

2 teaspoons instant coffee granules

2 teaspoons butter

1 cup (160g) icing sugar

1   Preheat oven to 160°C/ 40°C fan-assisted. Grease 14cm x 21cm loaf tin; line base and long sides with baking parchment, extending paper 2cm over sides.
2   Chop half of the nuts.
3   Stir butter, sugar, milk and coffee in small saucepan over low heat until smooth. Sift flour and cinnamon into medium bowl; stir in butter mixture, egg and chopped walnuts. Pour mixture into tin.
4   Bake loaf 15 minutes. Sprinkle with remaining nuts; bake further 30 minutes. Stand loaf in tin 10 minutes; turn, top-side up, onto wire rack to cool.
5   Make coffee icing; drizzle icing over loaf.
    COFFEE ICING Combine the water, coffee and butter in small heatproof bowl; stir in sifted icing sugar to form a firm paste. Place bowl over small saucepan of simmering water, stir until icing is spreadable.

Rhubarb & coconut loaf

preparation time 25 minutes   **cooking time** 1 hour 30 minutes   **serves** 10

1½ cups (225g) self-raising flour

1¼ cups (275g) caster sugar

1¼ cups (110g) desiccated coconut

125g butter, melted

3 eggs

½ cup (125ml) milk

½ teaspoon vanilla extract

1 cup (110g) finely chopped rhubarb

5 trimmed rhubarb stalks (300g)

2 tablespoons demerara sugar

1   Preheat oven to 150°C/130°C fan-assisted. Grease 14cm x 21cm loaf tin; line base with baking parchment.
2   Combine sifted flour, caster sugar and coconut in medium bowl; stir in butter, eggs, milk and extract. Spread half of the mixture into tin; sprinkle evenly with chopped rhubarb, spread remaining cake mixture over rhubarb.
3   Cut rhubarb stalks into 12cm lengths. Place rhubarb pieces over top of cake; sprinkle with demerara sugar.
4   Bake cake about 1½ hours. Stand cake in tin 5 minutes; turn, top-side up, onto wire rack to cool.

Glacé fruit loaf

preparation time 20 minutes **cooking time** 2 hours 30 minutes **serves** 12

185g butter, softened

½ cup (110g) caster sugar

3 eggs

1 cup (250g) finely chopped glacé apricot

½ cup (80g) finely chopped glacé orange

½ cup (90g) finely chopped stem ginger

¾ cup (210g) finely chopped glacé fig

1½ cups (225g) plain flour

½ cup (75g) self-raising flour

½ cup (125ml) milk

¼ cup (60ml) ginger wine

GINGER SYRUP

¼ cup (60ml) ginger wine

¼ cup (60ml) water

¼ cup (55g) caster sugar

2 teaspoons lemon juice

1 Preheat oven to 150°C/130°C fan-assisted. Line the base and both long sides of 14cm x 21cm loaf tin with baking parchment, extending paper 5cm above sides.

2 Beat butter and sugar in small bowl with electric mixer until just combined. Add eggs, one at a time, beating until just combined between additions; transfer to large bowl. Stir in fruit then sifted flours, and combined milk and wine, in two batches. Spread mixture into tin; bake about 2 hours 30 minutes.

3 Meanwhile, make ginger syrup.

4 Pour hot ginger syrup over hot cake in tin. Cover cake with foil; cool in tin.

GINGER SYRUP Stir ingredients in small saucepan over low heat, without boiling, until sugar dissolves; bring to a boil. Boil, uncovered, without stirring, about 2 minutes or until syrup thickens slightly.

Ginger wine, a beverage that is 14% alcohol by volume, has the piquant taste of fresh ginger. You can substitute it with dry (white) vermouth, if you prefer. Any type or combination of glacé fruit can be used in this recipe.

Apple raspberry bread

preparation time 15 minutes **cooking time** 1 hour 40 minutes **serves** 12

375ml jar apple sauce

1 cup (220g) firmly packed dark brown sugar

2 eggs

40g butter, melted

½ cup (125ml) buttermilk

¼ cup (90g) honey

1½ cups (225g) plain flour

⅔ cup (100g) wholemeal self-raising flour

½ teaspoon bicarbonate of soda

250g fresh or frozen raspberries

1 Preheat oven to 170ºC/150ºC fan-assisted. Grease 12cm x 22cm loaf tin; line base and long sides with baking parchment, extending paper 5cm over sides.

2 Combine apple sauce, sugar, eggs, butter, buttermilk and honey in large bowl; stir in sifted dry ingredients. Do not over-mix; mixture should be lumpy. Fold in raspberries.

3 Spread mixture into tin; bake about 1 hour 40 minutes. Stand bread in tin 10 minutes before turning, top-side up, onto wire rack to cool.

tips We used a chunky-style apple sauce for this recipe.
If using frozen raspberries, use them straight from the freezer as thawed berries will bleed colour through the cake mix.

Raisin & honey oat bread

preparation time 15 minutes **cooking time** 1 hour **serves** 10

1¾ cups (260g) self-raising flour

½ cup (110g) firmly packed brown sugar

⅔ cup (60g) rolled oats

1 cup (180g) raisins

2 eggs

½ cup (125ml) buttermilk

½ cup (125ml) vegetable oil

¼ cup (90g) honey

1 Preheat oven to 180ºC/160ºC fan-assisted. Grease 12cm x 22cm loaf tin; line base and long sides with baking parchment, extending paper 5cm over sides.

2 Sift flour into large bowl; stir in sugar, oats and raisins. Add eggs, buttermilk, oil and honey; stir to combine.

3 Spread mixture into tin; bake about 1 hour. Stand loaf in tin 10 minutes before turning, top-side up, onto wire rack to cool.

tip The bread will almost certainly crack; it doesn't matter, as most goodies baked in loaf tins will crack.

Chocolate beetroot loaf

preparation time 20 minutes (plus refrigeration time) **cooking time** 1 hour 30 minutes **serves** 12

3 small fresh beetroot (300g), peeled

250g butter, softened

1 cup (220g) firmly packed brown sugar

4 eggs

1⅓ cups (250g) dark chocolate chips

1 cup (150g) plain flour

1 cup (150g) self-raising flour

DARK CHOCOLATE GANACHE

100g dark eating chocolate,
chopped coarsely

⅓ cup (80ml) double cream

1 Preheat oven to 170ºC/150ºC fan-assisted. Grease 12cm x 22cm loaf tin; line base and long sides with baking parchment, extending paper over sides.
2 Grate beetroot coarsely (see tip).
3 Beat butter and sugar in small bowl with electric mixer until light and fluffy. Beat in eggs, one at a time (mixture might curdle at this stage, but will come together later).
4 Transfer mixture to large bowl, stir in chocolate chips and sifted flours in two batches, then beetroot.
5 Spread mixture into tin; bake about 1½ hours. Stand cake 5 minutes before turning, top-side up, onto wire rack to cool.
6 Meanwhile, make chocolate ganache. Spread cake with ganache.
DARK CHOCOLATE GANACHE Stir ingredients in small saucepan over low heat until smooth; transfer to small bowl. Cover; refrigerate about 40 minutes or until ganache is spreadable. Beat ganache with electric mixer until fluffy and paler in colour.

tips Wear disposable gloves when peeling and grating beetroot, as it will stain your skin.
Cake can be stored, in the fridge, in an airtight container, for a week, or can be frozen for two months.

Blueberry yogurt loaf

preparation time 20 minutes **cooking time** 1 hour 30 minutes **serves** 12

150g butter, softened

2 teaspoons finely grated lemon rind

1¼ cups (275g) firmly packed brown sugar

2 eggs

1¼ cups (185g) plain flour

½ cup (75g) self-raising flour

⅔ cup (190g) Greek-style yogurt

150g frozen blueberries

1 Preheat oven to 170ºC/150ºC fan-assisted. Grease 12cm x 22cm loaf tin; line base and long sides with baking parchment, extending paper 5cm over sides.
2 Beat butter, rind and sugar in small bowl with electric mixer until light and fluffy. Beat in eggs, one at a time. Transfer to large bowl; stir in sifted flours and yogurt, in two batches. Fold in blueberries.
3 Spread mixture into tin; bake 1½ hours. Stand cake in tin 5 minutes before turning, top-side up, onto wire rack to cool.

loaf cakes

Glossary

allspice also known as pimento or Jamaican pepper; available whole or ground.

almonds

blanched skins removed.

ground alonds are powdered to a coarse flour texture.

slivered cut lengthways.

baking powder a raising agent containing starch, but mostly cream of tartar and bicarbonate of soda in the proportions of 1 teaspoon cream of tartar to ½ teaspoon bicarbonate of soda. This is equal to 2 teaspoons baking powder.

bicarbonate of soda an ingredient of baking powder; also known as baking soda.

buttermilk fresh low-fat milk cultured to give a slightly sour, tangy taste; low-fat yogurt or milk can be substituted.

cardamom can be bought in pod, seed or ground form. Has a distinctive, aromatic, sweetly rich flavour.

cheese

cream a soft cow's-milk cheese with a fat content ranging from 14 per cent to 33 per cent.

ricotta a soft, sweet, moist, white, cow's-milk cheese with a low fat content (about 8.5 per cent) and a slightly grainy texture. The name roughly translates as 'cooked again' and refers to ricotta's manufacture from a whey that is itself a by-product of other cheese making.

cherries

glacé also known as candied cherries; boiled in heavy sugar syrup and then dried. Used in cakes, breads and sweets.

morello the dark, sour variety used in jams, preserves, pies and savoury dishes, particularly as an accompaniment to game birds and meats.

chilli, thai small, medium hot, and bright-red to dark-green in colour.

chocolate

chips hold their shape in baking.

dark eating made of cocoa liquor, cocoa butter and sugar.

milk eating most popular eating chocolate, mild and very sweet; similar in make-up to dark, but with the addition of milk solids.

white eating contains no cocoa solids, deriving its sweet flavour from cocoa butter. Is very sensitive to heat.

cinnamon dried inner bark of the shoots of the cinnamon tree. Available as a stick or ground.

cloves can be used whole or in ground form. Has a strong scent and taste so should be used minimally.

cocoa powder also known as unsweetened cocoa; cocoa beans that have been fermented, roasted, shelled, ground into powder then cleared of most of the fat content.

coconut

cream available in tins and cartons; as a rule, the proportions are two parts coconut to one part water.

desiccated unsweetened and concentrated coconut, dried and finely shredded.

shredded thin strips of dried coconut.

cornflour also known as cornstarch; used as a thickening agent in cooking.

cream we used fresh cream in this book, unless otherwise stated. Also known as pure cream and pouring cream; has no additives unlike commercially thickened cream. Minimum fat content 35 per cent.

soured a thick commercially-cultured soured cream. Minimum fat content 35 per cent.

whipping a cream that contains a thickener. Has a minimum fat content of 35 per cent.

cream of tartar the acid ingredient in baking powder; added to confectionery mixtures to help prevent sugar from crystallising. Keeps frostings creamy and improves volume when beating egg whites.

currants dried tiny, almost black raisins so-named from the grape type native to Corinth, Greece.

custard powder instant mixture used to make pouring custard; similar to North American instant pudding mixes.

date fruit of the date palm tree, eaten fresh or dried, on their own or in prepared dishes. About 4cm to 6cm in length, oval and plump, thin-skinned, with a honey-sweet flavour and sticky texture.

essences are synthetically produced substances used in small amounts to impart their respective flavours to foods. An extract is made by actually extracting the flavour from a food product. In the case of vanilla, pods are soaked, usually in alcohol, to capture the authentic flavour. Both extracts and essences will keep indefinitely stored in a cool dark place.

figs small, soft, pear-shaped fruit with a sweet pulpy flesh full of tiny edible seeds. Vary in skin and flesh colour according to type, not ripeness; when ripe, figs should be unblemished and bursting with flavour; nectar beads at the base indicate when a fig is at its best. Figs may also be glacéd (candied), dried or canned in sugar syrup.

flour

plain all-purpose flour.

rice extremely fine flour made from ground rice.

self-raising plain flour sifted with baking powder (a raising agent consisting mainly of 2 parts cream of tartar to 1 part bicarbonate of soda) in the proportion of 150g flour to 2 level teaspoons baking powder.

wholemeal also known as wholewheat flour; milled with the wheat germ so is higher in fibre and more nutritional than plain flour.

food colouring vegetable-based substance available in liquid, paste or gel form.

ginger

fresh also called green or root ginger; the thick gnarled root of a tropical plant. Can be kept, peeled, covered with dry sherry in a jar and refrigerated, or frozen in an airtight container.

stem fresh ginger root preserved in sugar syrup.

glacé fruit fruit such as cherries, peaches, pineapple, orange and citron cooked in heavy sugar syrup then dried.

golden syrup a by-product of refined sugarcane; pure maple syrup or honey can be substituted.

hazelnut-flavoured liqueur we used frangelico, but any hazelnut-flavoured liqueur is suitable.

hazelnuts, ground made by grinding hazelnuts to a coarse flour texture for use in baking or as a thickening agent.

macadamias native to Australia, a rich and buttery nut; store in refrigerator because of its high oil content.

maple syrup distilled from the sap of maple trees found only in Canada and parts of North America. Maple-flavoured syrup is not an adequate substitute for the real thing.

mascarpone a cultured cream product made in much the same way as yogurt. It is whitish to creamy yellow in colour, with a soft, creamy texture.

mixed spice a blend of ground spices usually consisting of cinnamon, allspice and nutmeg dried nut of an evergreen tree; available in ground form or you can grate your own with a fine grater.

orange-flavoured liqueur you can use any orange-flavoured liqueur: Grand Marnier, Cointreau, Curaçao are all suitable.

passionfruit also known as granadilla; a small tropical fruit, native to Brazil, comprised of a tough dark-purple skin surrounding edible black sweet-sour seeds.

pecans native to the United States; golden-brown, buttery and rich. Good in savoury and sweet dishes; especially good in salads.

pine nuts also known as pignoli; small, cream-coloured kernels obtained from the cones of different varieties of pine trees.

pistachios pale green, delicately flavoured nut inside hard off-white shells. To peel, soak shelled nuts in boiling water about 5 minutes; drain, then pat dry.

polenta a flour-like cereal made of ground corn (maize); similar to cornmeal but finer and lighter in colour; also the name of the dish made from it.

poppy seeds small, dried, bluish-grey seeds of the poppy plant. Poppy seeds have a crunchy texture and a nutty flavour. Available whole or ground in most supermarkets.

prunes commercially or sun-dried plums; store in the fridge.

rolled oats traditional whole oat grains that have been steamed and flattened. Not the quick-cook variety.

rosewater extract made from crushed rose petals; available from health food stores and speciality grocers.

semolina a hard part of the wheat which is sifted out and used mainly for making pasta.

star anise a dried star-shaped pod, the seeds of which taste of aniseed.

sugar

caster also known as superfine or finely granulated table sugar.

dark brown an extremely soft, fine-grained sugar retaining the deep flavour and colour of molasses.

demerara small-grained golden-coloured crystal sugar.

icing also known as confectioners' sugar or powdered sugar.

sweet potato fleshy root vegetable; available with red or white flesh.

treacle thick, dark syrup not unlike molasses; a by-product of sugar refining.

vanilla

extract obtained from vanilla beans infused in water; a non-alcoholic version of essence.

pod dried long, thin pod from a tropical golden orchid grown in central and South America and Tahiti; the minuscule black seeds inside the pod are used to impart a distinctively sweet vanilla flavour.

walnuts cream-coloured, wrinkled nuts with brown skin, formed into two distinct halves.

yogurt an unflavoured, full-fat cow's milk yogurt has been used in these recipes unless stated otherwise.

Index

Almonds
    Almond friands 80
    Almond honey spice cake 23
    Cherry almond loaves 103
    Orange, almond & pine nut cake 12
    Rhubarb & almond cakes 72
Apple
    Apple ginger cakes with lemon icing 78
    Apple raspberry bread 112
    Buttery apple cinnamon loaves 103
    Caramelised apple butter cake 27
Apricot
    Apricot & honey rock cakes 61
    Apricot loaf 92

Banana
    Banana & white chocolate chip
        cupcakes 62
    Banana bread 98
    Banana cupcakes with maple
        frosting 69
    Carrot & banana cake 14
    Chocolate banana bread 104
    Upside-down toffee date & banana
        cake 56
    Wholemeal banana & prune bread 107
Beetroot chocolate loaf 115
Berries (mixed)
    Berry cake with vanilla bean syrup 37
    Berry friands 80
    Berry muffins 86
    Gluten-free berry cupcakes 64
Blueberry
    Blueberry yogurt loaf 115
    Chocolate blueberry slab cake 50
Brownie bites, walnut 70
Butter frosting 29
Butter cakes
    Caramelised apple butter cake 27
    Vanilla butter cake 9
Butters
    Maple butter 95
    Whipped nut butter 104
Buttery apple cinnamon loaves 103

Caramel
    Coffee caramel cakes 75
    Ginger cake with caramel icing 32
    Whipped cream cake with caramel
        frosting 34
Caramelised apple butter cake 27
Carrot
    Carrot & banana cake 14
    Carrot cupcakes with maple cream
        cheese frosting 67
Cherry
    Cherry almond loaves 103
    Cherry syrup loaf 90
    Chocolate mud cake with chilli
        cherries 48

Chocolate
    Banana & white chocolate chip
        cupcakes 62
    Choc chip & walnut muffins 86
    Choc fudge cakes with coffee syrup 70
    Chocolate & hazelnut friands 80
    Chocolate & orange cupcakes 62
    Chocolate banana bread 104
    Chocolate beetroot loaf 115
    Chocolate blueberry slab cake 50
    Chocolate buttercream 75
    Chocolate coconut cakes 75
    Chocolate frosting 50
    Chocolate fudge frosting 89
    Chocolate fudge mud cakes 89
    Chocolate glacé icing 62
    Chocolate icing 29, 89
    Chocolate mud cake with chilli
        cherries 48
    Chocolate rum & raisin loaf 98
    Chocolate sticky date cakes 89
    Dark chocolate ganache 115
    Dark chocolate ganache 47, 48
    Family chocolate cake 50
    Flourless hazelnut chocolate cake 47
    Fudge frosting 50
    Lemon & lime white chocolate mud
        cake 53
    Mini chocolate hazelnut cakes 58
    Mocha cupcakes 62
    Raspberry & white chocolate friands 80
    Rich chocolate cake 29
    Rich chocolate hazelnut cake 47
    Walnut brownie bites 70
    Whipped hazelnut ganache 58
    White chocolate & macadamia cake 6
Cinnamon teacake 12
Citrus & poppy seed friands 80
Coconut
    Chocolate coconut cakes 75
    Coconut cupcakes 69
    Coconut ganache 53
    Lime coconut friands 80
    Moist coconut cake with coconut ice
        frosting 20
    Pineapple coconut cake 20
    Rhubarb & coconut loaf 108
Coffee
    Choc fudge cakes with coffee syrup 70
    Coffee caramel cakes 75
    Coffee glacé icing 62
    Coffee icing 108
    Coffee walnut loaf 108
    Mocha cupcakes 62
Cream cheese frosting 14
Creams
    Honey orange cream 23
    Mascarpone cream 54
    Orange ricotta cream 54
    Pistachio honey cream 11

Cupcakes
    Banana & white chocolate chip
        cupcakes 62
    Banana cupcakes with maple frosting
        69
    Carrot cupcakes with maple cream
        cheese frosting 67
    Chocolate & orange cupcakes 62
    Coconut cupcakes 69
    Gluten-free berry cupcakes 64
    Hummingbird cupcakes 64
    Mocha cupcakes 62
    Passionfruit & lime cupcakes 62

Dates
    Chocolate sticky date cakes 89
    Date & maple loaf 95
    Date & orange muffins 86
    Date, ricotta & polenta cake 54
    Upside-down toffee date & banana
        cake 56

Easy cupcakes 62

Family chocolate cake 50
Fig, pecan & maple syrup cake 43
Flourless hazelnut chocolate cake 47
Friands
    Almond friands 80
    Berry friands 80
    Chocolate & hazelnut friands 80
    Citrus & poppy seed friands 80
    Lime coconut friands 80
    Passionfruit friands 80
    Plum friands 80
    Raspberry & white chocolate friands 80
Frostings & icings (see also ganache)
    Butter frosting 29
    Caramel frosting 34
    Caramel icing 32
    Chocolate buttercream 75
    Chocolate frosting 50
    Chocolate fudge frosting 89
    Chocolate glacé icing 62
    Chocolate icing 29, 89
    Coconut ice frosting 20
    Coffee glacé icing 62
    Cream cheese frosting 14
    Fudge frosting 50
    Glacé icing 62
    Lemon icing 78
    Lime glacé icing 20
    Maple cream cheese frosting 67
    Maple frosting 69
    Orange glaze 77
    Orange icing 24
    Passionfruit glacé icing 62
    Passionfruit icing 37
    Pink glace icing 69
    Vanilla icing 97

Fruit cakes
    Chocolate rum & raisin loaf 98
    Glacé fruit cakes with ginger syrup 83
    Glacé fruit loaf 110
    Pineapple sultana loaf 104
    Raisin & honey oat bread 112
    Yogurt fruit loaf 100
Fudge frosting 50

Ganache
    Coconut ganache 53
    Dark chocolate ganache 47, 48, 115
    Whipped hazelnut ganache 58
Genoise sponge 9
Ginger
    Apple ginger cakes with lemon icing 78
    Ginger cake with caramel icing 32
    Ginger cakes with orange glaze 77
    Gingerbread loaves 97
    Glacé fruit cakes with ginger syrup 83
Glacé fruit cakes with ginger syrup 83
Glacé fruit loaf 110
Gluten-free berry cupcakes 64
Greek yogurt cake 17

Hazelnuts
    Chocolate & hazelnut friands 80
    Flourless hazelnut chocolate cake 47
    Mini chocolate hazelnut cakes 58
    Pistachio & hazelnut loaves 97
    Raspberry hazelnut cake 54
    Rich chocolate hazelnut cake 47
    Whipped hazelnut ganache 58
Honey
    Almond honey spice cake 23
    Apricot & honey rock cakes 61
    Honey orange cream 23
    Honey spice sponge cake 24
    Matzo honey cake 19
    Raisin & honey oat bread 112
    Spiced sponge with pistachio honey
        cream 11
Hummingbird cupcakes 64

Icings see Frostings and Icings

Lemon
    Apple ginger cakes with lemon icing 78
    Citrus & poppy seed friands 80
    Lemon & lime white chocolate mud
        cake 53
    Lemon poppy seed muffins 86
    Lemon sour cream cake 45
    Passionfruit & lemon syrup cake 39
Lime
    Lemon & lime white chocolate mud
        cake 53
    Lime & poppy seed syrup cake 30
    Lime & ricotta syrup cake 17
    Lime coconut friands 80
    Lime glacé icing 20
    Little lime syrup cakes 78
    Passionfruit & lime cupcakes 62

Macadamias
    Mandarin, polenta & macadamia cake 32
    White chocolate & macadamia cake 6

Mandarin, polenta & macadamia
    cake 32
Maple syrup
    Banana cupcakes with maple
        frosting 69
    Carrot cupcakes with maple cream
        cheese frosting 67
    Date & maple loaf 95
    Fig, pecan & maple syrup cake 43
    Maple butter 95
    Maple butterscotch sauce 43
    Maple pecan cake 43
Marble cake 29
Mascarpone cream 54
Matzo honey cake 19
Mini chocolate hazelnut cakes 58
Mocha cupcakes 62
Moist coconut cake with coconut ice
    frosting 20
Moist orange cake 24
Mud cakes
    Chocolate fudge mud cakes 89
    Chocolate mud cake with chilli
        cherries 48
    Lemon & lime white chocolate mud
        cake 53
Muffins
    Berry muffins 86
    Choc chip & walnut muffins 86
    Date & orange muffins 86
    Lemon poppy seed muffins 86
Muscat prune shortcake 40

Orange
    Chocolate & orange cupcakes 62
    Citrus & poppy seed friands 80
    Date & orange muffins 86
    Ginger cakes with orange glaze 77
    Honey orange cream 23
    Moist orange cake 24
    Orange blossom cakes 84
    Orange ricotta cream 54
    Orange syrup cakes 84
    Orange, almond & pine nut cake 12

Passionfruit
    Passionfruit & lemon syrup cake 39
    Passionfruit & lime cupcakes 62
    Passionfruit buttermilk cake 37
    Passionfruit friands 80
Pecans
    Fig, pecan & maple syrup cake 43
    Maple pecan cake 43
    Sweet potato & pecan loaf 92
Pineapple
    Hummingbird cupcakes 64
    Pineapple coconut cake 20
    Pineapple sultana loaf 104
Pistachios
    Pistachio & hazelnut loaves 97
    Spiced sponge with pistachio honey
        cream 11
Plum friands 80
Polenta
    Date, ricotta & polenta cake 54
    Mandarin, polenta & macadamia
        cake 32

Prunes
    Muscat prune shortcake 40
    Wholemeal banana & prune bread 107

Raisin & honey oat bread 112
Raspberries
    Apple raspberry bread 112
    Raspberry & white chocolate friands 80
    Raspberry hazelnut cake 54
Rhubarb
    Rhubarb & almond cakes 72
    Rhubarb & coconut loaf 108
Rich chocolate cake 29
Rich chocolate hazelnut cake 47
Rock cakes 61
    Apricot & honey rock cakes 61

Sauce, maple butterscotch 43
Shortcake, muscat prune 40
Spiced sponge with pistachio honey
    cream 11
Sponge cakes
    Genoise sponge 9
    Honey spice sponge cake 24
    Spiced sponge with pistachio honey
        cream 11
Sweet potato & pecan loaf 92
Syrup cakes
    Almond honey spice cake 23
    Berry cake with vanilla bean syrup 37
    Cherry syrup loaf 90
    Choc fudge cakes with coffee
        syrup 70
    Fig, pecan & maple syrup cake 43
    Glacé fruit cakes with ginger syrup 83
    Glacé fruit loaf 110
    Lime & poppy seed syrup cake 30
    Lime & ricotta syrup cake 17
    Little lime syrup cakes 78
    Orange syrup cakes 84
    Passionfruit & lemon syrup cake 39

Teacake, cinnamon 12

Upside-down toffee date & banana
    cake 56

Vanilla
    Berry cake with vanilla bean syrup 37
    Vanilla butter cake 9
    Vanilla icing 97

Walnuts
    Choc chip & walnut muffins 86
    Coffee walnut loaf 108
    Walnut brownie bites 70
Whipped cream cake with caramel
    frosting 34
Whipped hazelnut ganache 58
Whipped nut butter 104
White chocolate see Chocolate
Wholemeal banana & prune bread 107

Yogurt cakes
    Blueberry yogurt loaf 115
    Greek yogurt cake 17
    Yogurt fruit loaf 100

Conversion charts

measures

The cup and spoon measurements used in this book are metric: one measuring cup holds approximately 250ml; one metric tablespoon holds 20ml; one metric teaspoon holds 5ml.

All cup and spoon measurements are level. The most accurate way of measuring dry ingredients is to weigh them. When measuring liquids, use a clear glass or plastic jug with the metric markings.

We use large eggs with an average weight of 60g. This book contains recipes for dishes made with raw or lightly cooked eggs. These should be avoided by vulnerable people such as pregnant and nursing mothers, invalids, the elderly, babies and young children.

dry measures

METRIC	IMPERIAL
15g	½oz
30g	1oz
60g	2oz
90g	3oz
125g	4oz (¼lb)
155g	5oz
185g	6oz
220g	7oz
250g	8oz (½lb)
280g	9oz
315g	10oz
345g	11oz
375g	12oz (¾lb)
410g	13oz
440g	14oz
470g	15oz
500g	16oz (1lb)
750g	24oz (1½lb)
1kg	32oz (2lb)

liquid measures

METRIC	IMPERIAL
30ml	1 fluid oz
60ml	2 fluid oz
100ml	3 fluid oz
125ml	4 fluid oz
150ml	5 fluid oz
	(¼ pint/1 gill)
190ml	6 fluid oz
250ml	8 fluid oz
300ml	10 fluid oz (½ pint)
500ml	16 fluid oz
600ml	20 fluid oz (1 pint)
1000ml (1 litre)	1¾ pints

length measures

METRIC	IMPERIAL
3mm	⅛ in
6mm	¼in
1cm	½in
2cm	¾in
2.5cm	1in
5cm	2in
6cm	2½in
8cm	3in
10cm	4in
13cm	5in
15cm	6in
18cm	7in
20cm	8in
23cm	9in
25cm	10in
28cm	11in
30cm	12in (1ft)

oven temperatures

These oven temperatures are only a guide for conventional ovens. For fan-assisted ovens, check the manufacturer's manual.

	°C (CELSIUS)	°F (FAHRENHEIT)	GAS MARK
Very low	120	250	½
Low	150	275-300	1-2
Moderately low	160	325	3
Moderate	180	350-375	4-5
Moderately hot	200	400	6
Hot	220	425-450	7-8
Very hot	240	475	9

This book is published by Octopus Publishing Group Limited based on materials licensed it by ACP Magazines Ltd, a division of PBL Media Pty Limited

54 Park St, Sydney
GPO Box 4088, Sydney, NSW 2001
phone (02) 9282 8618;
fax (02) 9267 9438
acpbooks@acpmagazines.com.au;
www.acpbooks.com.au

OCTOPUS BOOKS

Design: Chris Bell
Food Director: Pamela Clark

Published and Distributed in the United Kingdom by Octopus Publishing Group Limited

Endeavour House
189 Shaftesbury Avenue
London WC2H 8JY
United Kingdom
phone + 44 (0) 207 632 5400;
fax + 44 (0) 207 632 5405

aww@octopusbooks.co.uk; www.octopusbooks.co.uk
www.australian-womens-weekly.com

Printed and bound in China

International foreign language rights,
Brian Cearnes, ACP Books
bcearnes@acpmagazines.com.au

A catalogue record for this book is available from the British Library.

ISBN 978-1-903428-01-6
© ACP Magazines Ltd 2010
ABN 18 053 273 546

To order books:
telephone LBS on 01903 828 503
order online at www.australian-womens-weekly.com
or www.octopusbooks.co.uk